THE SHADOW DANCERS

By

Ernie Bein

© 1999, 2002 by Ernie Bein. All rights reserved.

No part of this book may be reproduced, stored in a retrieval system, or transmitted by any means, electronic, mechanical, photocopying, recording, or otherwise, without written permission from the author.

ISBN: 1-4033-1601-5 (e-book)
ISBN: 1-4033-1602-3 (Paperback)
ISBN: 1-4033-3570-2 (Dustjacket)

This book is printed on acid free paper.

1stBooks – rev. 11/19/02

THE SHADOW DANCERS

CONTENTS

Chapter One	Joseph the Carpenter	1
Chapter Two	Simon Peter	20
Chapter Three	Matthew - The Tax Collector	34
Chapter Four	John	51
Chapter Five	Thomas The Twin	73
Chapter Six	Mary Magdalene	95
Chapter Seven	Nicodemas	113
Chapter Eight	Simon the Zealot	126
Chapter Nine	Zacchaeaus - the Chief Tax Collector	140
Chapter Ten	Mary - A Samaritan Woman	156
Chapter Eleven	Judas	170
Chapter Twelve	Caiaphas - the Chief High Priest	187

INTRODUCTION

What would Simon Peter have to share with us, if he were in our midst today? What would his testimony be? What would Mary Magdaline or the woman at the well, or Joseph the carpenter who took a pregnant woman to be his wife, have to tell us. What would the hated Judas Iscariot have to say about his relationship with Jesus?

What would their testimonies be?

That is a question that has invaded my prayer life for many years.

This book is the result of the study and meditation created by that question. It is the me, the mind and spirit, that Jesus created!

This book is about the people who danced in the shadow of Jesus Christ. It is about those very human men and women who walked with him and knew him. Some for many years. Some very briefly. Some from a distance. Some intimately. This is not an attempt to sanctify them. It is an attempt to understand and learn from them.

Each has a lesson of faith to teach us.

What is found on the pages of this book is not traditional in its interpretation. It is scripturally sound and essentially far more historically and scholastically defensible than much of our tradition. The scholarship we have had available, but seem determined to ignore, tests and defies many of our traditional understandings. Understanding the time and place of Jesus' ministry confirms, more than denies, his divinity and humanity.

It does not resonate with recent attempts to rewrite history and scripture in order to sanctify theological and sociological biases. Unlike what has come from radical liberal pens, this is not an attempt to throw out all that has been a part of the faith since the beginning. It is rather, an attempt to better understand it.

There have been resources available for more than half a century that clearly show the strong probability that Jesus was a Pharisee.

The belief systems, theological understandings, use of scripture, concern for a faith lived out in daily life, and a deep attention to the well being of the people are all things shared by Jesus and the party called Pharisee. His familiarity with sitting in the Moses Seat, which was reserved for the Pharisee Rabbi, suggests he was one. Jesus differed from them on some major points, best explained by Jesus moving beyond the legalism that tried to fine tune life, to an expression of a loving, forgiving relationship as the basis for faith.

If Jesus was indeed a Pharisee, the gospels must be read differently than we have ever read them in the past. He becomes one serving God from childhood, instead of a person whose lifestyle was radically changed for some unknown reason. Similarly, those he gathered to help in his ministry are no longer strangers he snuck up upon and pulled away from their lives as some mysterious explosion of religious fervor. Suddenly the gospels become far less confusing and far more human.

When I began to read the Bible seriously, I questioned all that we have held dear about the villain Judas. Most scriptural references to him don't fit our ideas of Judas. Reason and scripture challenge our traditional attitude about him. My approach to the study of Scripture has not relied upon accepted interpretations. I began to read and study with an attitude of discovery. I searched for more. The contents of this book reflect that search.

This book is not written to take issue with any theological perspective or belief system. My primary thesis is simple: the more we know about the world in which Jesus ministered and the people around him, the better we are able to apply what he taught to our own lives.

This book is fiction.

I have taken a few imaginative paths. The Samaritan Woman might have been the woman who anointed Jesus at Simon's house, but I admit that is a stretch. The places where I have taken imaginative directions never violate the scriptural description of who and whose these persons were, or the historic facts of how life was in those times.

Chapter One

Joseph the Carpenter

THE WITNESS:

Joseph was a middle aged man of 28. (In his time and place in history, the life expectancy of a man was 40.) He was a skilled carpenter and had a better than average income. He was a very well respected person in the community. He had always lived in Nazareth. There were only 24 families in this little village. Much of Joseph business was with the travelers along the Roman Road that ran past Nazareth to and from Ceasarea by the Sea and Capernium. Marriages were arranged and there were very few choices in such a small village. Ten years earlier he paid dowry and was betrothed to the four year old daughter of a good family of Nazareth. He had patiently waited for her to achieve the age of marriage. A devout Jew, he had remained celibate, awaiting his marriage bed. He was an elder in the local synagogue, which was very small. When there was no Pharisee (Rabbi) to pastor the congregation of the synagogue, Joseph would teach the children Hebrew and the lessons of faith, and take turns teaching in worship. Unlike the region of Galilee, which had only an 11% Jewish population, Nazareth was 100% Jewish. This was a very close and homogenous community. Joseph was known throughout the region as an honest business man and a fair person.

THE TESTIMONY:

My name is Joseph.

I am a carpenter.

I work with wood.

Sometimes with stone or metal.

Ernie Bein

I make things.

I learned my trade from my father and he from his father.

I have looked forward to sons of my own to teach how to be carpenters.

It is good to pass down to a child what you have learned in your life.

To pass down things a child will use in his life.

The skills are important.

But beyond that, it is important to make sure your sons and daughters understand the important lessons of living.

I long for sons and daughters of my own to raise up straight and true like a tall cedar.

So that they may live lives that glorify God and continue the heritage of Israel.

These are difficult times.

Our nation is tax poor!

Taxes are so high that many who owned land for generations have been forced to sell, and then live as day workers, many times working the very fields that once were their family's.

We live in a region that is dominated by foreigners.

It is hard to keep the Jewish Jewish.

Our little town has huddled together to keep things as they should be.

THE SHADOW DANCERS

But matters of faith are harder to keep safe than they were years ago.

Satan is sending new temptations to our children every day.

It is important for the children to know the scriptures and the prayers, and to know how to doven and chant.

It is important for them to love God first and their neighbor as themselves.

Only then will they be able to live well in these troubled times.

I am pleased to be able to teach at the synagogue from time to time, when there is no Rabbi.

I also have been able to teach the children their Hebrew and lessons of faith, when there is no Pharisee - Rabbi -to lead us.

The Pharisees are our teachers - our Rabbis.

They are craftsman, like myself, so they can make a living where ever they live.

They have been educated in the Law and Prophets and teach us how to live, day to day, as God wants us to live.

They are good men.

Very good men.

But they sure have a lot of rules to follow.

It is very hard to be righteous as they define righteousness.

Only they are allowed to sit in the Moses seat.

Ernie Bein

When I teach I stand since I am not due the respect they are accorded.

But they sit, and all of us stand to hear their teaching.

Usually they never marry, since their lives are committed to the service of God and man.

Having a family and children is a big job.

It is the duty of a Jewish man to see to it his children are raised with love and respect for God and man.

A Pharisee cannot serve two masters, God and a family.

So most of them do not marry.

They do not always stay in the same place long.

Their time in one place is especially short in small villages, like ours.

So we have a teacher for awhile, then we make do until another comes.

The Pharisees, - the Teachers - are our life line to God.

The Priests in Jerusalem care not at all about the people.

They would die to protect the Temple, but turn their backs on the misery of the people.

The building and things are more important to them than the people.

The Pharisees teach us to observe the holy days and do all that scripture requires of us for the proper observation of our feasts and sacrifices.

THE SHADOW DANCERS

They ask more of us.

They expect us to live our lives like God's people.

Every day!

They expect us to be different than others.

Every day!

Better than others.

Every day!

Every single day!

Being a carpenter in Galilee is a good life and a good living.

I serve my town with my skills.

It is fun making things for my friends.

I serve strangers traveling on the Roman Road with my skills.

I get to meet new people every day as they travel back and forth on the Roman Road.

They wait while I work on what it is they need.

So we get to share some time and talk.

I learn much about the world I will never see from them.

Sometimes they let me tell them about the God they don't know.

Being a carpenter is a good life and a good living.

Ernie Bein

A new axle or wheel for the cart of some traveler.

Some piece of furniture or a new plow for one of my friends in town.

Or maybe a new house for a newly betrothed couple.

I am always busy making something for someone.

Or I am off selecting and cutting the wood to be used later after it has seasoned.

The most popular wood is cedar. But there aren't many of those trees left around here anymore.

I use a lot of fir and some oak.

I need help when I cut and haul the oak.

Oak is substantial, and very, very heavy.

I like what I do.

I like the sweat of hard work on my face.

I like the way working causes my body to weary and the ease with which I rest at night.

I like the feeling that doing a good job gives me.

I like what I do.

In a land where prosperity has disappeared, I make a good living.

I have accumulated a decent amount of wealth.

My house was my father's house.

I have redone it twice since the death of my father.

It is better than any other in town.

Amos, the potter does well, also.

All of us who are craftsmen have a better life than those whose only skill is in tending the fields.

If you don't own the field, your living depends on the whim of the land owner or the steward.

If you are your own boss things go better.

The truth is that the only persons who can accumulate any money are the very wealthy, who had it in the first place, and the craftsmen who work hard and earn it every day.

Everyone else is constantly on the verge of starvation.

If someone could learn to multiply food so that a few morsels were enough to feed thousands of the "People of the Land" they would be worshipped as a god.

Or followed as the one to defeat the Romans and make us free again.

And the talk of revolution would slow greatly, if not cease altogether.

Those are the politics of our times.

The politics of an oppressed people.

We are used to that.

Much of our history has been spent under the rule of foreigners: - heathens, - you know *GENTILES*.

Ernie Bein

I don't know why God loves us more than them, but I am glad he does.

But oppression is only a surface problem.

Those whose lives are in the hands of God will never be less than who they are.

No soldier or tyrant can ever change that.

We are directly touched by Roman rule only a little here in our village most of the time.

But now Rome has greatly interfered with my life and it will cost me most, if not all, of my life savings to do what they have ordered.

More about that later. I'm getting ahead of my story.

It all started ten years ago.

I was looking for a wife, but there weren't any prospects in our village of marrying age.

We have tried to keep within our village.

That way we only marry Jewish and the faith will be kept as it should.

Our women will have a husband to care for them after their fathers die.

A single woman in our society has no status, no living, no future.

There are only two ways for a single woman to support herself if her father has not left her with great wealth.

She can beg or she can become a prostitute.

We must marry within our own community, lest any of our women are left to such dire circumstances.

I am from a leading family in town. So my dowry was large. The fathers of our village were anxious to arrange for me to marry their daughters. I was considered a good catch.

All of the marriageable women were already married.

All of the older girls approaching the age of marriage were betrothed, that is committed to marry someone.

There were several who were still quite young whose fathers approached my father.

There was one who was very young, only four, who was presented to me by her father.

Actually she was presented to my father first and then to me.

She was a sweet child from a very good family.

Her father was devout and an elder in the synagogue.

I had confidence she would be raised as a faithful servant of God.

She was a very good choice for me.

But I would have to wait many years before we could marry.

All things considered, I felt she was worth the wait.

So the dowry was paid and the agreement was made.

We were betrothed.

She really didn't understand then what that meant.

She has been raised to know that when she was old enough she would be my wife.

Over the years we have grown in friendship and then love.

I have been blessed by her every time I have seen her.

She has grown in grace and spirit.

She is a beautiful woman.

We didn't speak for many years.

It would have been unseemly to have done so.

But as she grew older it was polite for me to nod or greet her when we met.

Or when she passed my shop, as years went by she did that more and more, she would tilt her head and show a shy little smile as she nodded as she passed.

She was a part of the girls class I taught Hebrew and the lessons of Israel at Synagogue.

We got to know what each other was like in a distant and polite way then.

She seldom spoke. Her smiles and dancing eyes acknowledged her recognition of me and the special place I had in her life.

As she grew, I grew in my admiration for her. She was such a lovely and dear child.

She is very bright.

We are a multi - lingual culture.

Every devout Jew must know Hebrew.

Our day to day language is Aramaic.

To converse with those traveling the Roman Road we must speak Greek.

She could speak Greek, Hebrew and Aramaic fluently by the time she was seven.

Her numbers and her market skills were developed very early.

At a very young age, she could sew and had all the household skills a woman needs.

Her father said she was ambitious about being a good wife.

Her father shared with me how she was growing in her faith. She was a devout girl, attending to her prayers, participating in family worship and assisting during special holidays like the Passover.

Her love for God and her goodness became a legend in our town.

I became more and more pleased with the prospects of sharing a home and life with her.

I began to love as God has taught to love.

It became clear to me I would sacrifice anything for her.

I would give up my life for her.

I didn't believe there was anything I would not do to please her.

Then a year ago it was proper for me to begin courting her.

I would dine with her family.

Ernie Bein

She would cook.

Her mother wanted to show off what a good wife she would make, so Mary did all the things at table a wife should do.

I would go to the well to see her early in the morning when the women came to draw water.

Once in awhile we would be allowed to be alone and we would walk, hand in hand about the village.

The towns folk would smile and nod as we passed.

The love we shared

- the love that had grown over the years

- the devotion to each other

- that I thought was so private

- had been obvious to the others.

It seemed the whole town was as happy about us as were we.

Everyone seemed to be patiently waiting for our marriage.

I have never been filled with such joy as was I then.

Sometimes at night we would go up on the roof of her father's house and look at the stars.

With her mother to chaperon, of course.

The sky was always beautiful for us.

Watching the stars became very special for Mary and me.

There is something about the night sky that will always be very special for us.

Our nights are very chill. She would curl up with her back against my chest and I would wrap my arms around her against the cold.

Those were wonderful times.

Then my world was crushed.

My Mary was pregnant and I knew it was not my child!

It could not have been my child.

The dreams of over one third of my life were shattered. The beautiful woman who was pledged to me had lain with another.

I was so deeply hurt!

I felt so betrayed!

How could she have done such a thing?

She knew how I adored her.

I thought she loved me too.

Was I too old for her?

Did she really care for some younger man?

Was all I had seen in her eyes just my imagination?

Was everything she said a lie?

I have never been more miserable -

Ernie Bein

I have never doubted my self value more!

I have never felt so hopeless as when I got the devastating news of Mary's pregnancy!

I doubted everything about us.

Women who commit adultery in our culture are stoned.

A woman who is betrothed and who lies with another man has committed adultery.

If I admitted we had not been together, she could be stoned to death, along with the child she carried.

In an angry moment I thought about doing that.

But my love for her was too strong to do anything to hurt her.

There was some story her father told me that was ludicrous.

She claimed God was the father of her child.

God is the father of all of his children.

God does not make babies with women. That is blaspheme.

I was offended that she would create such a story to claim she had been faithful.

Even her father didn't believe it.

If I quietly divorced her - that is - put her away - then her father could keep the dowry, but she would remain a part of his household.

He, then, would be responsible for her and the child.

She could not, of course, stay in Nazareth!

It would be necessary for her to go live with relatives.

She has a cousin, Elizabeth that lives near Jerusalem. She could go and be with that family.

I would never marry.

My honor would always be questioned.

I would be suspected of having dishonored her.

Life was truly dismal and I had no future.

Then things changed and I was given truth.

Truth that was unbelievable.

Have you ever seen an angel?

I have!

Just when everything I cared about was shattered, God spoke to me and joy dawned again.

True joy is an ultimate sense of well being.

I have the most ultimate of ultimate senses of well being!

It is a sense that life is good and I will be blessed by God no matter what the rest of the world thinks or does.

What Mary had said was true!

The child she carries is no ordinary child. She is to be the mother of the Messua.

Mary, the woman I had grown to love, had been chosen by God to be the most blessed of all women.

The angel came to me at night and told me the story.

He even gave me a name for the boy.

I rose up immediately and went to the house of Mary's father and awoke them all.

"I am here to take my wife to my home!" I announced.

Her father grinned and her mother wept.

She simply walked to me and I took her hand.

On the way home she asked, "God has spoken to you?"

"Yes"

She slept curled safely in my arms that night and every night since.

We talked about all of this often since.

We are filled with joy that is beyond imagination at what God is doing with and through us.

Mary's time is getting closer and Rome has caused us discontent.

Rome is requiring everyone to be registered.

They require this registration to be done in the city that is the seat of the tribe.

I am of the House of David. I must go to Bethlehem to be registered.

I must take my wife with me.

That is a long and hard journey for a pregnant woman.

I will have to make a lot of special arrangements.

I will need a beast of burden for her to ride upon.

A donkey will be a smoother ride than a camel.

Either will be better than a hard, bouncing cart.

I have a precious cargo to transport.

We will have to stop and rest often.

It is unsafe to travel alone, one must always be in a group of travelers.

I will have to buy into a group in order to travel with them.

We may start with one group of travelers, but it is not likely we will be able to keep up with them.

Probably we will be with several groups before we reach Bethlehem.

I will have to buy into each group. This will be a costly trip.

She may make it there before the baby is born, but she will never make it back to Nazareth.

I will have to find a place to settle in Bethlehem for a year or two.

It is not good to try to transport young babies and new mothers.

So we will stay in Bethlehem for a time.

Ernie Bein

I will have to close up my house here. It will be secure until we come back home.

This is going to be very costly.

Fortunately, I have some wealth to rely upon.

We will be able to afford to stay at inns along the way and when we first get to Bethlehem.

I can afford to purchase a good donkey.

I will carry my tools with me, so I can earn my living there in Bethlehem for as long as we need to stay.

It will take time to get my business established there, so we will have to live on my savings for a time.

Our means will be skimpy, but we will be all right.

If things go easily,

- if the baby doesn't come until I have had a chance to get established

- if I can have a comfortable home for him and his mother

- then things will be fine.

Even in a different place.

Things will be fine.

Even then we will exhaust our financial resources and it will be difficult until I get my business going.

But we know that no matter what happens, God is in charge.

THE SHADOW DANCERS

We are going to be all right no matter what goes on around us.

We don't know all that is going to happen to us, but God does.

That is all we need to know.

WHAT A JOYOUS TIME IS THIS!

Chapter Two

Simon Peter

THE WITNESS:

Simon Peter was a successful business man in the major industry of the Galilean area - fishing. He was well known and well thought of in Capernaum. He was as transparent as the air, as impulsive as a two year old, opinionated, bright, perceptive and simple in taste and habit. He had a special spiritual quality that was, at times, betrayed by his impulsive nature. He was a devout man who had been loyal to the faith. Jesus was the resident Pharisee - Rabbi - at the Synagogue where Peter worshipped. Peter's home was right across the alley from that Synagogue and across the Roman Road from the Olive Press and the Wine Press that nestled together against a gentle hill as the Roman Road headed up the little hill and out of town. It was a prestigious and busy place for the home of a prestigious and busy man.

THE TESTIMONY:

I am a simple man.

I have always been a simple man.

I have worked hard, treated people well, and had been honest in my dealings. I had always kept my word.

I have done well.

Life was good. Very, very good. I had a good wife, great children and a fine home. I had a thriving business and good partners.

Life, indeed, was very good!

THE SHADOW DANCERS

I was a fisherman. A very good fisherman. I loved fishing. Galilee was a very good place to fish. The work was hard, but that was a part of what I loved about it.

It was pleasing to me to feel the power of my muscles against the weight of the nets; to sweat in the sun as I mended nets, repaired the boats and dried the fish. I liked to work in the boats in the cool of the evening, bringing in the catch, until the same sweat oiled my body. Then - when ever the thought struck me - to dive into those pure blue waters and feel the poison of the work draining from my body.

Those soothing, cooling waters.

How I loved my little sea.

My sea teemed with life. The best eating fish in the whole world came from my sea. Rome feasted upon dried Galilean fish.

Most of which **I** provided.

Well, **all right, a lot** of which I provided.

All right! Me and my brother and my partners, the Zebedees.

We provided it.

Andrew and I loved working with the Zebedees, James and John. They were our friends.

Good Friends.

I had always had a lot of good friends - men I had grown up with there in Capernaum. Men I had played with when we were boys. Men whose children I had cuddled and at whose weddings I had danced.

Good friends.

Ernie Bein

I have had only one enemy in my life.

Oh, I have lost my temper and shouted at people. At times I even cursed people. But they knew me. I got over things quickly. I never had any long lasting problem with anyone. Of course, I wish I hadn't gotten so excited so easily. I said and did things for which I was sorry. People forgave me.

Now my little brother Andrew, he took his time and thought things out. He would lay his hand on his beard and stroke it with great tenderness. You just knew he was thinking things over. Then, when he said something, you **knew absolutely** he had thought it over and you listened carefully.

But me, I just blew off.

The fact that I was usually right didn't change the fact that I made a fool of myself too often to be happy about it.

I wished I had learned to keep my mouth shut. Even when I was right. I wished I had been more like my little brother. But I was not.

And the folks around Capernaum put up with my faults with grace.

I had a lot of friends.

You know - a friend is someone who knows all about you and loves you anyway.

Well, I had a lot of them.

But I had one enemy!

Matthew the traitor!

Matthew the Tax Collector!

THE SHADOW DANCERS

Matthew grew up with us. Played with us. When we were younger he celebrated with us at the very first wedding we went to after we achieved manhood. He had been my very best friend.

But I grew to hate him!

The sight of him rubbed a raw place on my heart. I wore cotton and he wore linen. My clothes were of one color. His were of many colors. As well as I had done, he had done better. Mine came from the honest sweat and ache of my muscles and from the wise understanding of business my father had taught me. His came off the backs of his former friends. From betrayal and treachery! He cheated and robbed his own people.

He was a Tax Collector for the Roman heathens!

I wanted nothing to do with a man who betrayed his own friends, his own family, his own people. Yet, I had to see him every time we made another shipment of fish to Rome. Which was about every other day. I had to pay him money on what my hard work and honest business had created.

Mathew was my enemy and that was the only thing in my life that was not good!

He was a disgrace to all Jews.

I had always been a good Jew. I had tithed and celebrated the feasts. I had been to Jerusalem seven times for the high holy days at the Temple. I had been in Synagogue every Sabbath for most of my life. I had been looked upon as an Elder in my congregation. It was not by accident that I built my house across the alley from the Synagogue. I knew my prayers, and could flex and doven to the shame of others who could not stay in time with me. (I think some of them just didn't have any rhythm - they couldn't dance as well as me either.) I had read the scrolls often in worship. I had been considered a leader in our congregation. An Elder.

Ernie Bein

Oh life was good.

Very, very good!

But there had always been something missing for me. You know, some piece that wasn't there. A little hole inside me that never ever got filled. No matter how hard I worked; no matter how happy we were at home; no matter how many friends I had; or how much respect I received from folks; there was always something missing in my life.

Until I got a new friend.

He was a carpenter and a Pharisee. He didn't grow up in Capernaum. He came from Nazareth to Capernaum when his brother James was ready to take over the carpenter's shop in Nazareth. His home was near mine and he was very skilled with wood. We shared a lot of good times. Just being with him was a good time.

He did most of the teaching at our Synagogue. That is what the Rabbi - the Pharisee - did, you know. There was always something special about his teachings - about him. It was kind of confusing. Like - he had the key to what was missing in my life.

Then he got in the way of my good life!

Seriously in the way of my good life!

Then things got turned upside down.

EVERYTHING GOT TURNED UPSIDE DOWN.

Andrew had gone down the Jordan Valley to the Ford of Bethbara to listen to the teachings of an Essene who was causing a lot of excitement.

Like I said before, Andrew was deep. He thought things out a lot. Didn't say much, but thought a lot.

He had made several trips and had followed the Essene for awhile, listening to his teachings and sitting at his feet.

This Essene was of a priestly family, a Levite and he was causing a great stir.

He had started preaching to the travelers who went across the little ford in the Jordan. It was a busy place. It was where the Roman Road crossed the Jordan River. So many, many people were there every day. People began to talk about what he was preaching and others who were not travelers began to go out just to hear him. They said he might be the ONE. He began to draw great crowds.

He was pretty smart. Beside having a captive crowd to begin his teaching at the crossing, he had some water there so he could baptize people for repentance.

He really didn't like the shallowness of the water there. You had to get a lot closer to the Sea of Galilee to get shoulder high water in the Jordan River. He was an Essene you see, and had been used to the deep water at Qumran for that sort of thing. At Qumran he used to wash himself for his sins seven times a day in these pools they had there.

Seven times.

He sure must have sinned a lot to have to do that.

Later he went to the mountains where there was deeper water to baptize while **we** were baptizing at the Ford of Bethbara on the Jordan. Now I am getting way ahead of this story.

This last time, Andrew came home with some disturbing news. He said that Jesus, our resident Pharisee and carpenter of excellence, our friend and the most human man I knew, was the ONE.

The long awaited Messiah.

Ernie Bein

And of course, when Andrew said something like that I listened. We all listened. That got even ME to think before I said anything. We all thought about all of that. We thought a lot about it, and talked a lot about it.

We talked it over with the Zebedees in the boats and on the shore constantly.

A few months later Jesus came by where we were working. The nets were wet and needed drying. They also had some holes in them that needed to be repaired. We were busy, but he didn't care. He had more important business and he wanted his friends to help. He had a crowd with him and he was teaching. Then, finally, he addressed us.

"Follow me and I will make you fishers of men" he said.

I didn't have the slightest idea what he meant by that. I did know that the most important thing in my life was to do what he asked. No matter what that might be. So me and my brother Andrew and the Zebedees left our boats and followed him.

My wife didn't really understand.

I couldn't explain it!

I didn't understand myself!

How could I explain it to her!

The folks who bought our fish got angry.

We just up and left it all.

James' and John's dad tried to keep things going with hired help. But they never could do what we did.

THE SHADOW DANCERS

It effected a lot of people close to us and people who depended on us.

It was a choice between good and very good. I never had a lot of trouble deciding between good and bad. But most of the important choices of life are not between good and bad. They are between bad and worse or good and better.

No other person can understand or make those choices for you. You have to make them yourself.

Jesus called us.

We had to answer right then and there.

We did.

That good life - that very good life - was left behind. The funny thing is I was happier and more satisfied with myself than I had ever been in all of my life.

That empty spot was gone!

But to tell the truth I almost lost it all - I almost turned right around and left when he walked right up to Matthew at the Tax Table and asked him to come too. It was very hard to forgive the treachery of a man I had grown up with. When someone you had called friend betrays you it is hard to forgive. **Because you don't want to forgive!** What I wanted to do was to hurt him as much - no - more than he hurt me!

It worked out.

You see, Jesus' presence and love for both of us made the difference. It really made *all* the difference.

In the end, Matthew and I were as good friends as we had been as children. I learned a lot about forgiveness. I found out that as long as I tried to forgive I couldn't! When I let Jesus do it in me, it was easy. People who talk about how hard it is to forgive try to do it themselves. They never let God do it. They keep control and so they fail. Well, that was just one of many lessons I learned those next three years.

At first there was a lot of supernatural stuff.

Blind folks got their sight.

The sick got healed.

Cripples walked.

The possessed were set free.

Even the dead were alive again.

Then there was that day on the mountainside. A few fish and some bread multiplied into enough to feed that whole crowd. I thought my eyes were doing funny things in the Galilean sun. When I tried to pick up a fish it became two. Then four, then eight. I was speechless!

No one of **this** world can do those kinds of things. He was the ONE all right.

Some people never got past the miracles. Some people never got past expecting him to do some more of them. Some more exciting, supernatural things.

These were hard times. Economically tough times. Most of the people here lived as day workers. They didn't get much money. They got a great deal of hard work. But they didn't get much money. When they did get work, which wasn't every day, it was back breaking labor. They had their own dreams about what it would be like in the Kingdom of God. So they were really excited with the miracles - and so some of them missed the real stuff.

A lot of them did.

I guess most of them did.

The times that were the best for me were the nights. Out in the open most of the time, we learned as he talked to us in the evenings or at night. Laying around the fire with the stars and the moon in the sky and the cool evening air, he taught. He taught us so much at those times. That is when he explained the parables the people didn't understand.

That we didn't understand.

We began to understand.

That is when we began to hear things that were beyond our imagination. That is when life was best of all for me.

The very best of all.

That time at Philippi was like that. Only better. The spring fed pool at Philippi is a good place to be. The mountain wall is straight up for a hundred feet. There, about twenty feet up the wall, the water seeps out of the stone. It pools underneath. That pool is clear and sweet. This was the source of the upper Jordan River.

It was a gathering place. Our time there was as clear and sweet as the water. We were resting near the pool when he said "Who do they say I am?" We told him. He just kind of smiled that all knowing smile that half says he is being patient with the ignorance and foolishness of people because he loves them anyway. He didn't do that in an arrogant or judgmental way. He just sort of mused over knowing things that no one else could guess.

Anyway, that is how it started. Then he got down to serious business. He got real serious. He asked "Who do you say I am?" We all knew the answer. We all knew who and what he was. We had all known for a long time.

Ernie Bein

But the others were nudging me. "Go on Peter, go on and tell him."

I get so excited, sometimes, that I would just about explode and the heat of emotion came out of my mouth in a rush of words.

Often the others encouraged me to speak up. They might have been a little wiser than I, and knew when to keep their mouths shut.

No.

They **were wiser** than I.

Keeping quiet and letting someone else speak up. That was something I had never learned to do. At times I have been really embarrassed by my quick mouth and slow brain. Like the time I chastised him for talking about dying. Well, after all, that sort of thing was against everything I had ever learned about the Messiah. I had always been taught the Messiah could not, would not die. Should not die.

Jesus really got angry. He told me to go to hell!

I was shocked and hurt.

I knew I should have kept my mouth shut that time.

I really knew.

Again, when he said that I would deny him I didn't even consider what might be going on later, or what the situation that might be. So I got my mouth in the way again.

I had to eat my words.

I **bitterly** ate my **bitter** words and was brought to my knees with that one.

I was afraid and I didn't understand what was happening.

So I tried to protect myself.

And I denied my Jesus.

You know, that is what gets in our way every time. We try to protect ourselves. We forget his power and promise. We try to take care of ourselves. The self preservation thing gets in our way - hurts our ability to follow him.

I wasn't bothered with that stuff after the resurrection. I couldn't keep my mouth shut after that either. But then I wasn't afraid any more. Then I spoke with the power of the resurrection in my heart. Then I looked the people in the eye who had crucified Jesus and told them what they had done and what the penalty was going to be for them.

I was fearless.

As a matter of fact, my big mouth was never a problem after that.

You see, then I had something important to say. Something worth saying. Something Jesus wanted them to hear. Things that, at times, were beyond my own understanding

So my greatest weakness became an asset.

I guess I got ahead of myself again.

Well, getting back to Phillipi.

The answer was easy. "You are the Christ!" I said.

He was pleased with my answer. He was so happy when I had those words of faith and revelation!

That was a great time. One of the times I think was best of all. If there is any time I like to remember, that is probably the one.

But then I have a lot of great memories.

If I have anything to be embarrassed about in my memories, it is my inconsistency. I kept letting myself get in the way of all the marvelous stuff. I could shine one minute and go dark the next.

I was walking on water one minute and got scared and was sinking the next.

When I could forget me, then I did fine.

When I couldn't, I always failed.

When I failed, Jesus was always there to bail me out, or help me out, or straighten me out.

I sure have had some marvelous moments with Jesus.

Special ones, that are unlike anything anyone else has had.

After all, none of the rest of those guys ever walked on water. -

Even when I failed, I knew that there was nothing in life worthwhile without Jesus.

He is my friend.

My mentor.

My leader.

My Savior and Lord.

Despite all of my mistakes, he still has important plans for me.

He has important things for me to do.

As I think back over it all, one thing strikes me.

As good as life was, as very good as ever life was,

I never dreamed of how good it was going to get, when I laid down my nets, gave it all up and followed Jesus.

Chapter Three

Matthew - The Tax Collector

THE WITNESS:

Matthew was the Capernaum Tax Collector. He was a Jew. He had collected taxes from Peter, Andrew, James and John as they exported fish. He grew up in Capernaum with them and others, whom he betrayed as a collaborator with the oppressing Romans. Although he tried to rationalize his decisions, he gave up self respect and his relationships with all other Jewish citizens for wealth and material goods. He was a sinner by everyone's standards but his own. He came into painful reconciliation with God and God's people through his relationship with Jesus Christ. He was a traitor and sinner who was called to follow Jesus.

THE TESTIMONY:

Capernaum was a great place to grow up.

There cannot be any place where the grass is greener, the sky or the water are bluer, or where the air is sweeter.

There has always been a lot of excitement and activity in Capernaum.

The Roman Road runs right through Capernaum as it connects the world with Rome. Every day there were travelers coming through our city. Camels, asses, oxen and occasionally a horse loaded down with merchandise or pulling loaded carts, traveled through our town daily, heading one way or another.

People from all over the world passed through our city regularly. I used to like watching them. Many of them dressed funny.

Most of them spoke funny languages, although everyone spoke Greek. It was all right if they had their languages. We had our Hebrew and Aramaic. We all had to learn Hebrew as children so we could understand our heritage. It was the language of the Synagogue. But only Jews knew it. Everyone spoke Aramaic who lived in Galilee. So we actually had two languages that were ours. We thought in Aramaic most of the time so we were a little slower speaking Greek than we were speaking Aramaic. If we really wanted to confuse everyone else about what we were saying we would speak Hebrew.

It was like sitting by the edge of the road and watching the world walk by.

I spent a lot of time after harvest by the side of the Roman Road as it turned north out of town, at the wine press by the Synagogue. My father had a large vineyard. He pruned and trimmed his way into the best producing vineyard in Galilee. I loved to go with him to the wine press and watch people while he worked.

Capernaum was a wonderful place to grow up.

I enjoyed Capernaum.

I enjoyed growing up there.

I enjoyed growing up as the son of a grape grower.

A vineyard was a wonderful place to play. Our vineyard was sprawled across some of the many beautiful hill sides around Capernaum. It would take nearly all day to walk through all of the vineyard with my father, checking the vines, occasionally tasting the grapes to see if they were sweet and ripe yet.

Sometimes my father and I would just sit at the top of a hill and look around.

At the vineyard.

Ernie Bein

At the beautiful wildflowers across the corner of the sea.

At the serene blue water of the sea.

At the blue cloudless sky full of birds.

At the people moving along the road below.

Sometimes we would just sit there and enjoy the sun and the occasional breezes.

I enjoyed the vineyard.

I enjoyed growing up in that vineyard.

I had such a great group of friends as I grew up. Jimmy and that selfish little Johnny. Phil and Bart. Andy and Si. Si was my best friend. He was so funny. So carefree. I had a great time playing with him. I had a great time growing up with him. My friends used to love to run through the vineyard with me. To hide behind the vines and jump out at each other. Life was fun growing up in the vineyard of my father.

I enjoyed growing up there.

I enjoyed having my friends there.

Every once in a while we would meet at our favorite spot on the sea and go swimming. We might swim all afternoon and fish a little in the evening as the sun was going down. Then we would build a little fire and cook our fish. No other food ever tasted as good as our fish cooked by the side of the sea with friends.

We had a great time together, no matter what we were doing: - playing - fishing - swimming - or studying Hebrew at the Synagogue.

We were inseparable.

THE SHADOW DANCERS

We grew up together.

I enjoyed growing up with those guys.

I guess I grew up in the greatest place with the greatest people I could imagine.

At least, that was what I thought as I grew up. I had no sense of the misery of many of our people during those first years.

My innocence eroded slowly. I was having so much fun I didn't notice. Simon did. By the time we were men, I understood very well what was happening to most of those whose families had farmed the land for centuries.

Most of these were people living on the Plain of Sharon and the Jordan Valley. So they weren't neighbors and it took awhile for the news to travel. Taxes on the land were so high that with even the best possible crop every year, they struggled to survive. So they began to sell their land to aristocrats who had the money. When the money from the sale ran out, they had to work in the fields they once owned. It all seemed tragic - but a bit far off.

I was a man and married before it hit our family. We became like many others. Bad times and taxes destroyed our way of life.

After three years of draught, the grapes were small and dry and they didn't make wine. Times had gotten more difficult. Income had been reduced to nothing. But the taxes on the land continued. Then it happened. It was all over. The vineyard was gone. Sold to someone who lived somewhere else and had his steward in charge.

The money we received for the vineyard was not very much and it went quickly.

My father got a job as a vine dresser. I did too. But our fine house began to need repairs that couldn't be done.

Ernie Bein

Simon offered to let me work for him on their boats as an extra job when they didn't need me as a vinedresser in the vineyard in which I grew up.

I got bitter.

All my dreams, all my joys, all of the things I loved were gone. My life was sour. Like the dry juiceless grapes on the vines, all the fruit of my life was worthless. I resented the success of my good friends. I became jealous of them.

The local Tax Collector was killed. He was found with a Jewish dagger - a sicarea - in between his third and fourth ribs. There were reprisals and men were executed. None of my friends were among them. They were all day workers - People of the Land. That was the group from which came the revolutionaries who called themselves Zealots. So the Romans killed twenty of them. Crucified by the Roman Road so everyone could see their naked bodies being picked apart by the vultures.

It was a double horror.

The first horror was to be humiliated by being naked and exposed to the eyes of all. The second was to be tortured to death. It was a terrible way to die. The Romans meant for it to be terrible. They were sending a message to anyone who might be considering rebellious acts against them. The consequences of rebellion were clear.

It was a terrible time in the city of my childhood.

A terrible time.

Then the Chief Tax Collector decided he wanted a Jew to be the Tax Collector for Capernaum.

He thought it might be less likely that the local people would kill one of their own.

It was not unusual, in order to better their circumstance, for Jews to capitulate with the foreigners who ran our country. The party called Sadducees, who mostly lived in Jerusalem and were Levites, were all capitulators. They ran the country.

They even changed our calendar to agree with the Roman Calendar. Now we celebrated our Holy Days in confusion. Those who refused to give up our Hebrew calendar always celebrated things a few days earlier than the official national day of celebration. Many of us celebrated Passover on our Friday, which was the Roman Tuesday

Of course a Tax Collector was considered a sinner and a traitor. Tax Collectors were shut out from the Synagogue, and religious celebrations. They were hated by all Jews. But I had so many good friends I never dreamed that would happen to me.

It was a very good living, to be a Tax Collector. There was a base amount that the government got. But then the Tax Collector could collect what ever he wanted. Double, triple or even ten times the amount the government got could be demanded by the Tax Collector.

They all got very rich very quickly.

I wondered if a person could not be a good Tax Collector and treat people well.

Not gouge them.

Collect only what was fair.

I wondered if a good person could not make a necessary evil less painful for the people.

I thought that I could be as good a Tax Collector as anybody.

Down deep I was probably rationalizing. In the back of my mind was the thought of the revenge I might take. I thought about what I could do to the new owners of our vineyard, if I controlled the taxes on it.

So I took the job.

I tried to tell Si and my friends how I was really doing everyone a favor. They wouldn't listen. Immediately I became the enemy of every citizen of Capernaum. I was aware of what people thought of Tax Collectors. I really didn't think I was being a traitor to my people. I thought that I could be a good Tax Collector, taking only what was fair, that I could treat people fairly and they would appreciate it.

Wrong!

I have an orderly mind. I had kept accounts for the vineyard. So I took well to the tax collection business. I kept the tax accounts very, very carefully. I was in charge of tariff on business as well as the land tax. I felt better about taxes on merchandise than on land.

Greed was a slow, but very strong, seductress.

The adding of a little more here for this luxury, or a little more there for another, and pretty soon I was getting just as much as any other Tax Collector. If everyone hated me, there was no reason to be nice to them.

It was their own fault.

I began to accumulate things. Nice things. Nice clothes. I began to dress well. So did my family. I was becoming wealthy in the land of my birth that was filled with suffering, hunger and poverty. That which had ruined my father and had caused so much misery in my land was the source of my wealth.

In a matter of three years I put the vineyard out of business and it got broken up into little plots of useless hillside before I was finished with it. If it was not ours it would be no one's My father was dead now. I didn't want it any more.

After I became a Tax Collector my father just sort of quit trying to live. He didn't eat. He just sat by the sea and looked out into nothing.

One day he died.

I told myself he was weak and couldn't handle life as well as I.

I knew he was ashamed of what I was doing.

All he had left, after the vineyard was gone, was the family honor and dignity.

I had taken those away from him.

In a very real sense, I felt superior to my father and others who had been brought low by the Taxes. I had proven I could take that which destroyed others and make it work for me.

I got paid back for what I got in ways I thought I would avoid. The place I felt it most was at the Synagogue. When I tried to attend worship I was met at the door by Si and the others who had been my friends. I was a sinner. I could not desecrate the sanctity of Synagogue with my presence.

I got more and more bitter and took it out on those who had been my friends. I wanted to make them sorry they treated me that way when they brought their merchandise through my Tax Post. They paid a high price for their unkindness.

Literally!

Then it happened.

When I enjoyed nothing in life!

When I was at my bitter worst.

Ernie Bein

At my loneliest.

At my most discouraged, lowest point.

At the time I hated myself and nearly everyone else.

That is when it happened.

I was standing at the Tax Post, collecting the tariff as usual. My friend Jesus, the carpenter, came up to my table. I knew him well and loved him. He was the only thing in my life that wasn't a mess.

Unlike everyone else in town, he was always kind to me. I always carefully made sure his taxes were minimal. We talked a lot when I could find him home or sitting by the sea. Sometimes he would just smile and listen. He was our teacher at the synagogue. So even if I couldn't worship, I got some private time with the one who always had the right answer.

Sometimes he said things to me I really didn't like, but he was always right.

He was always kind.

He was the only friend I had left in Capernaum.

He was the only respectable person who treated me with respect.

He was the last link I had to my Synagogue too.

He just walked up, interrupted my collections and said "Follow me!"

He didn't say where.

He didn't say why.

He didn't say for how long.

THE SHADOW DANCERS

If I hesitated it was because I had a table full of money and several persons waiting to be taxed.

He didn't even blink when I gathered up all I could in my pouch and followed. He just sort of smiled that smile of his that said, "Oh well, maybe some day you will learn." and walked off with me right behind.

I hated leaving all the rest of that money there. I hated to leave people standing in line who could just walk right through without being taxed. I heard later that people hurried to get things through before another Collector could be appointed. Since I never bothered to officially resign, there were a lot of taxes lost. There was also a lot of confusion for the Chief Tax Collector who became very angry.

I didn't care.

The worst part was leaving my family. They heard about it all second handed. I know that they were both angry and proud. Angry because I had just up and left. Proud because my life was different and I wouldn't be an outcast anymore. That all of the family wouldn't be outcasts any more.

He had already started teaching outside of the Synagogue, in the fields and on hillsides.

I had gone to listen to his teaching with a growing number of others. There were a lot of folks who had begun to say special things about him. A lot were following him wherever he went. He began to pick some of us to be more than just disciples. We were to be his inner circle of close friends and to represent him at special times and places. I wasn't the first he had chosen. I was not the last either.

There was a problem between me and my former friends who had already been chosen. Jesus helped us get past that. It was more than a little tense when Si and the gang saw he was bringing me along. You could have cut the air with a sicarea, it got that heavy, when I was with the rest.

Si nearly screamed at Jesus and pointed to me. "How many times must I forgive - seven times seven." Jesus knew what we were all thinking. How could we be close to him when we were so hostile to each other? I thought I was more wronged by them than they by me. But that was how they felt. "No - seventy times seven!" Jesus answered.

The numbers were symbolic. It was like saying "Keep forgiving until you don't have to anymore."

I started with myself and got serious.

I began to ask myself what had I done wrong.

Never mind my good intentions.

Never mind how I rationalized my actions.

Didn't they really have something of consequence against me?

Had I not really treated my friends badly.

So I went to Si. I confessed my sins against him and begged forgiveness - on my knees. I pleaded with him to forgive me. Si was a big guy. A really big guy. His legs looked like a couple of barrels. I just curled my arms around his legs and cried.

He cried too.

What a sight - to see that big man with tears running down his cheeks. I only saw him cry like that once more. Later. On that special Sunday morning.

He fell on his knees and hugged me and asked me to forgive him for what he had said and done to me. Pretty soon the whole gang was crowded around me and we were crying and being blessed beyond our wildest dreams.

Jesus picked twelve of us to be his closest friends and to share his ministry.

Some others were already selected and were there with Jesus and us when it all happened. Jesus, Judas, the Zealot and James looked on with differing expressions. Jesus glowed. Judas and the Zealot looked less than impressed. Little James looked more bewildered than anything.

It was a great day. I got my friends back.

I got my life back.

We were beginning a most glorious adventure.

We were in the midst of the most important events of all time.

We were a part of it together and now we had a larger group of close friends to share it with.

Life was good again.

If I enjoyed Capernaum and all that it had meant to me, I enjoyed even more what we did together.

I enjoyed life again.

I loved Jesus more than anything.

I will always marvel at the way loving Jesus helps erase the barriers between people. I did things with and because of Jesus that were beyond anything imaginable.

When we got sent out two by two I was paired with Judas.

Ernie Bein

Judas was my new friend. Actually that money I took with me from the Tax Post got put in the treasury. My new friend Judas took care of the treasury.

As I was saying, wondrous things happened when we were sent out two by two. We laid hands on sick and blind people and they were healed.

I laid hands on a sick little girl with her parents and the whole village watching. I knew she would be healed. I felt heat in my hands and she felt a very hot place where I had my hands. My arms and hands trembled and I knew things were happening through me that I never dreamed possible. I was praising God and calling for her to be healed in the name of Jesus. We both felt some strange sensations. Eyes brighten. She sat up. She asked for something to eat. Later she stood up and hugged her parents. People were crying and praising God. Then she hugged me and I cried. I never knew I could do something as worthy and good as all of this. Jesus and the Holy Spirit he kept talking about gave us that power.

PRAISE GOD!

We were attached by a demoniac. Judas looked him right in the eye and said - "In the name of Jesus Christ be gone - leave him." The man fell to the ground and started to twist and roll.

Judas wasn't giving up.

He was a stubborn man, determined to have his way.

He **screamed** "In the name of Jesus Christ be gone!" There was a loud rushing noise like wind and the man lay still. I reached down and gave him my hand and the man stood up, clear and sound and praising God.

If a man had never been a part of something like that, he would never believe it!

Or ever understand it!

I found that the more I believed and had faith the more things of marvel and consequence happened with and through me. Life wasn't only good, it was important!

We came back from that trip so filled with joy and peace I didn't think anything would ever make me unhappy again. One day I found out that happiness and joy are different things.

We were making a difference in the world. Because of Jesus the world would never be the same. We were a part of that.

What could be wrong with that?

I was overjoyed.

Sometimes, when we sat around a fire by the sea and cooked fish, or slept on a hillside with the stars over us, it was like when we were children. It seemed like all the very best of what was and the fullest hope for what would be, were gathered in our hearts and minds at those moments.

Times were going to get difficult. The crowds didn't want to hear about loving enemies and being humble. So they drifted away, still looking for what was already there.

Trying to find the ONE they had already met.

Who would have ever believed what happened to us.

Who would have expected that Judas would get so caught up in his own agenda, that he would do what he did.

Who would have ever thought that Si, who we were all calling Peter by then, would have denied even knowing him. He didn't fool anyone. He spoke, as do all of us, with the Galilean brogue. There is a gentle burr in the voice of all who grew up in Galilee. Everyone knows a Galilean by his speech.

"I don't know him!"

Everyone in Galilee knew Jesus. Three times he lied, and everyone knew he was a liar.

We were frightened also and hid without a word. It seemed that all at once we were scattered and our dreams were gone. We found each other back at the upstairs room where we had spent that last evening with him.

Then he found us and life turned sweet again.

We went back to Galilee and met him for the final time.

Final time in this world.

That was all right, because now we knew this is not all there is.

We knew absolutely that we would live forever.

Nothing on earth held any power over us any more.

He gave us the marching orders of our faithful journey.

"All authority in heaven and earth has been given to me.

Go therefore and make disciples of all nations, baptizing them in the name of the Father, the Son and the Holy Spirit, teaching them to observe all that I have commanded you; and lo, I am with you always."

Always!

Not just for a life time in the terms of this world, but always!

Forever!

No end!

I could always do anything, when Jesus was with me. To the ends of the earth.

All my good friends and I went different directions. Doing what each of us was called to do in his name. Knowing that we would all be together again later.

The Sanhedrin got very nervous about the disappearance of Jesus body. So they paid the soldiers to lie. They said we had stolen it.

Right!

That would mean we were lying about the most important thing in life - life eternal.

Only an idiot could imagine we were so willing to suffer and die to perpetrate a lie about life after death.

Not one of us changed his story to save his life.

We would never have been so steadfast had we been lying.

Anyone with the sense of a blind camel would understand that our lack of fear of death - after the resurrection, not before - was proof of what we said.

Look at what a tremendous change there was in Si - I mean Peter the Rock - after the resurrection compared to before it, during Jesus trial!

We were more than followers now.

We were ambassadors to the world for God himself.

Ernie Bein

After the resurrection - not before!

All else had been preparation.

I have used my orderly mind and ability to keep good records and wrote an account of the most important things that happened. I wrote for those who believed, but hadn't seen it all.

I didn't try to write everything. I would not be on this earth long enough to do that. Just those things that were important, so people would believe and know his lessons.

I enjoyed writing about it all.

More than anything I have ever done.

I really enjoyed it.

I really, really enjoyed it.

Chapter Four

John

THE WITNESS:

John was a very young and a very spoiled teenager. He was precocious and very lovable. As a teenager, he had assumed the responsibilities of a man. He worked with the men in the boats with an equal load to pull. Good humored and quick witted, he was fun to be around. He was a practical joker who kept those around him laughing. He had a hard time getting past his selfishness and preoccupation with what he wanted. These things stood in the way of his loving others, since he was always focused upon what they can do for him and never upon what he can do for them. He learned to love because Jesus had loved him and called him to become more than he had been - to give up what he was for what he could become.

THE TESTIMONY:

My big brother, James, was seven years older than me.

It didn't seem like very much after we were grown up.

It certainly did when I was a child.

My earliest memories are of following my big brother around, frequently to his dismay. I used to tag after him and all his friends.

Simon and his brother Andrew were a part of that gang.

There was only two years between Simon and Andrew. They kind of grew up together. I envied that.

We all became partners in the fishing business, but they never let me forget what a pain I had been and still was.

In a way, they all kind of asked for it.

I was a cute kid.

I used to make them all laugh, and they gave me what I wanted. I learned early that if you can keep people laughing they don't mind you being around no matter how self serving you are.

I learned to work them for everything I wanted or thought I needed. When nothing else would work and I didn't get my way, I whined a lot.

Everyone was a lot happier when I was happy.

Sometimes I would play tricks on the older guys.

Funny little things.

Like putting beetles on the grapes in the bowl from which they were eating.

Once I put sheep dung in Matthew's clothes when they were all swimming.

Another time I tied all their clothes up with rocks inside and threw them in the sea when they wouldn't let me swim with them.

I hid and laughed at them as they all ran home naked.

In our town naked is not good.

They were so embarrassed.

In Matthew's vineyard, I thought of all sorts of things to do with grapes.

Most of the time they laughed it off.

Sometimes, however, I went too far and they took a long time to smile.

Our father was a very successful fisherman. He had three slaves - we usually referred to them as servants. One woman was a house servant. The other two were men who helped in the boats.

We did very well and the man power was important to our family. With that many servants and their families in our household, I got a lot of attention.

They all loved me!

I was a cute!

I also had three older sisters. Since I was the youngest in the family, I generally got a lot of attention from the girls too.

I had very attentive parents.

I really had it soft.

Some might say I was spoiled.

My father had a partner in the fishing business from the time he first began.

His name was John and I was named after him. They were very good friends.

John's sons, Simon and Andrew became our father's partners when they became men because of the age of their father, John. He would go down to the shore and help them with the nets from time to time, or greet them when they came in from fishing

Ernie Bein

James had a lot of friends his age, who I followed around.

There were always those older guys to stick up for me, take care of me and even pamper me.

I had servants, parents and sisters to dote on me.

I knew I was very special.

I had to be.

Everyone treated me very special.

So I had to be!

I really was a cute kid!

As soon as I was old enough, I joined my brother and father in the boats.

I may have been spoiled and self centered, but I wasn't lazy. Working with the men actually made me feel grown up and more special.

I had a great time at the expense of my brother and our friends in the boats. I was always pulling a joke on someone. Most of the time my jokes keep everybody happy.

There was one time I was very happy and no one else was.

I carefully and intentionally looped the anchor rope loosely between his feet and around Simon's leg. When the anchor was thrown out the rope tighten and it slipped around his leg.

He was so big I never thought it would pull him overboard.

It did.

He lost his balance and fell more than was pulled.

But overboard he went!

What a big splash he made!

I was in deep trouble.

Both Andrew and James had to dive in to help him get loose.

When I saw the trouble I caused, I decided that I really needed a swim.

So I dove in, on the shore side, and just kept on swimming.

I laughed to myself all the way to shore.

I was beyond the anger I had just created, and I thought the funniest sight I had ever seen was the expression of Simon's face as he went under the water.

I went home before father and James did and hid from them.

I was really very nervous about things with everyone in the boats for a long time after that.

I kept expecting Simon to get even.

Actually, they all got even!

They all got even, but not the way I expected. Have you ever been in boats for hours at a time, day after day, and week after week, with people who would never speak to you?

It was a long time before they spoke to me at all, and then for a long time only about things that needed to be done in the boats.

I guess I was supposed to learn my lesson.

But I didn't.

A fish in Simon's or James' clothes while we were fishing always got a reaction when they put their clothes back on.

I enjoyed fishing.

By the time I was fourteen I was able to do everything any older man could do.

I was doing well enough so that our father could stop fishing and my brother and I took the boats out.

He was usually there when we were working on the beach or coming in from the catch. He was slowing down and it was time for him to take his ease. Just like John, his old partner, had, before he died.

It felt good to be helping my brother run our part of the business. As the oldest son he was, of course, in charge. I felt important because he would talk things over with me and explain things so I understood why he was doing things the way he was.

Our partnership was very good.

Simon had the best business mind and was the most skilled of all of us, so he was kind of in charge of the business.

Our two slaves had grown older with our father so most of the time they worked with us just on the shore.

It was good being one of four partners in the most successful business in Capernaum.

It made me feel important.

Special!

Very, very special!

I was pretty proud of how well I had done and was doing.

I was just as special, as a fifteen year old, as I had been as a child.

The person that made me feel the most special was our teacher at the Synagogue.

I liked hearing from him about how God loved me. He told me I was a unique creation of God; different and special, created for a special purpose.

In the late afternoon, before we put the boats out, when he was finished with his work in his carpenter shop, we would all just sit and talk.

Sometimes along the shore, resting in the sun.

Sometimes at his shop.

All four of us would talk about and to him.

Of course Simon and James had to describe every nasty little trick I ever played on them. They hoped he would chastise me.

Most of the time he laughed.

Sometimes he just twitched that left eye brow at me and stared as if to say "Will you ever grow up and be a man."

He never *said* a word.

He just listened.

One morning, after we had fished unsuccessfully all night, we were all mending nets and washing them and our boats. Father and the servants were there. It was late in the morning and we were about finished. Jesus called to us and asked our help.

He was just down the shoreline about twenty cubits.

There were a lot of people who had followed him there.

They were crowding in too close for him to teach.

I watched and wondered if they might accidentally do him harm as they pressed against him.

He called to Simon for help.

Simon put their boat in the water, went down to where Jesus was and he got in the boat. Simon rowed it out far enough so Jesus could teach safely.

James, Andrew and me walked down to where they all were to listen.

I sat there with my feet in the water seated on the softest spot I could find among the stones and rocks.

Oh yes, I knew you were supposed to stand while the Rabbi sat and taught.

The teacher would take the place of honor, seated in the Moses Seat, while everyone else stood out of respect.

I figured out a good excuse, though.

I rationalized that this wasn't the synagogue and the boat seat wasn't the Moses Seat Jesus usually sat upon.

I used to call the Moses Seat, in a very good humored manner, "the throne of judgment and grace" because the Rabbis always told us about God's judgment upon his people and his grace and mercy because we were his people.

The Moses Seat really was made like a sort of a throne.

Jesus taught for about half an hour while sitting in Simon's boat. Then he did something that was very strange.

"Put out in deep water and put down your nets." he told Simon.

I was amused.

He had a good sense of humor.

We all knew that.

This had to be a joke.

We were professionals and very good ones. We had spent all night fishing with only a pitiful few fish to show for our hard work. Night time was always the best fishing. You could never catch much in mid morning. Fish were not active then. They are active and feeding at night, early morning or late evening. Night was always the best. We took most of our clothes off when we worked the nets and that was also a reason nights are better. It was more private at night since it is dark and no one can see. It was cool and more comfortable then.

Now here was our carpenter friend telling us how to fish.

He didn't really give people a lot of foolish orders.

He was a great *carpente*r.

We were great **fishermen** and he was telling us how to do our business.

We would never have told him how to make a table!

This just had to be some kind of joke!

Simon only had one of his nets in the boat. The others were on shore drying. One still needed to be mended. That was, after all, what we were doing when he came by. So I didn't think there could possibly be any fish caught in this little tabloid.

This was anything but a joke!

When Simon threw his net where Jesus said and started to bring it in, there were more fish in that net than I had ever seen being caught at one time.

Simon called to us. Andrew, James and I ran back to the other boat, threw all the other undamaged nets in it and pushed off.

Andrew took the rest of their nets and jumped into the other boat with Simon and Jesus.

We all struggled for about two hours bringing in the huge catch. We crossed over and re-netted and re-netted again. We pulled in one net full of fish after another until our boats were dangerously low in the water.

It took all of the skill we had as fishermen to bring in that catch!

We saw him differently then!

He wasn't just a great teacher and good friend.

He got our attention as he had never done before!

His power to do the miraculous had been demonstrated to us, as to no one else.

As professional fishermen we understood better than any of the spectators what he had done and how impossible it was.

THE SHADOW DANCERS

This was for **us.**

This miracle was to tell **us** something!

So we would know, beyond any doubt who and what he was.

He wasn't just our local Rabbi any longer.

Then he talked to us about being "fishers of men."

So we left it all and followed him.

We left it all: family, friends, business, home town - all.

All of it!

I was pleased that, as he was beginning his traveling ministry, he chose me as one of his apostles.

That means I was chosen as one of the special twelve who were his personal representatives to all of the world.

I was one of his ambassadors to represent him to others. It was a very important thing, to be a part of the inner circle of the special people of Jesus.

There were thousands of people crowding every place he went in order to see and hear him. It was exciting as he moved from place to place with all those people following.

There were always a lot more along the road, or in any town we went through.

They would call out.

They would try to touch.

Ernie Bein

They stared at and cheered us. What a great feeling to be a part of all of that.

One day we had taken him from Gerasa on the east coast of the Sea and had landed near Tiberias. As usual, a great crowd immediately gathered and pushed in around. We tried to help give him some space, but weren't very successful.

Jairus, the leader of the local Synagogue dropped on his knees in front of Jesus and begged him to help his sick daughter.

We were on our way to Jairus' house when a woman pushed right past me and touched the hem of Jesus cloak.

She was a frail thing and very pale. She didn't hang on him and backed right off right away. I didn't have to do anything to get her out of the way.

I was impressed with the peace that came over that wretched, drawn face.

That pitiful, pale face.

Her eyes came alive and her thin lips curled in a strange smile. I wasn't sure exactly what had happened, but I knew something had.

Jesus knew power had been drawn from him and asked about it. I helped her back to him. She had - ah - um - bleeding - um - ah - female trouble for twelve years! It is a surprise she hadn't bled to death.

Doctors had done everything they could for her, but she only got worse.

She said she knew she was cured. Healed by touching Jesus clothes.

THE SHADOW DANCERS

Jesus looked at her with those dear, compassionate, loving eyes and said "Your faith has made you well, go and suffer not more."

She looked at him with eyes sparkling from those deep hollow sockets with a joy for life and love for Jesus that stirred me.

I thought I had just seen the most impressive healing miracle I would ever witness. But like the morning Jesus told Peter to drop his nets in deep waters, I had no idea of what would happen next.

Oh, I'm sorry. That is what we were calling Simon by then - Peter - the rock. Jesus gave him that name at Caesarea Philipi.

You see, in our tradition, when a person's life is radically effected by God and he becomes a leader in the plan of God, his name is changed by God. Abram became Abraham. Jacob became Israel. Simon became Peter.

Jairus' servants came and said that the girl had died.

That should have stopped us.

It didn't!

Jesus took me and Peter and James and we hurried with Jairus to his house.

The mourners were gathering and beginning to wail when we got there. Jesus said "She is just asleep" and they laughed.

The mourners scoffed and whispered. I could never understand how people could like making a living being sad. I have always been suspicious of mourners.

He dismissed them!

Sent them home!

Told them they were no longer needed!

When Jairus nodded, they walked away, very quiet, and very resentful!

He took the parents and me and James and Peter into where she was. He ran all the rest of the wailers out.

He spoke to the dead twelve year old daughter of those two weeping parents!

Can you imagine?

He began talking to a dead child!

Right in front of her grief stricken parents!

Either he was the most arrogant and audacious man who ever lived, or he was the Son of God himself.

He said, in the strongest, most forceful voice I have ever heard him use, to her, "Little girl, I say to you **get up**!" The resonance of his voice caused me to tremble.

He took her hand and she stood, walked over to her parents and hugged them. She smiled at us.

My knees were weak and my mouth was dry and hung open. I could not believe I had just seen what I had just seen!

My stomach churned and I thought I was about to disgrace myself.

I couldn't believe what I had just seen happen!

Yet I knew it really did happened and I knew I was a part of the most wonderful things this world had ever seen or would ever see.

THE SHADOW DANCERS

Jesus looked at her and her parents in a caring, loving, satisfied way that made my heart ache with joy.

He had a special smile.

His shoulders were square and his head tilted slightly to the left side with that eyebrow doing what it frequently did.

I wondered if there wasn't a kind of glow about him.

Jairus and his wife and their daughter stood together and all three looked at him with so much more than gratitude.

They stared at the life giver,

the compassionate lover of people,

the one who hurt when others did and felt their pain more deeply than even they themselves did.

What I saw in their eyes was joy beyond gratitude.

I saw peace.

I saw a love that was beyond anything I yet had known.

I guess I felt resentful.

I perceived something between them I did not have with Jesus.

It hurt to think anyone had something with Jesus I didn't.

Maybe he didn't love me the most after all.

I got a lot of attention from folks because I was with him.

Especially when we were on a mountain side and he was teaching.

Ernie Bein

I noticed the envy in the eyes of others my age who saw me as a part of this group of important men, all of whom were older than me. I was one of the people considered special by him. I really felt special when he gave me the power of the Holy Spirit to heal the sick and cast out demons.

People sure admired me for helping them.

I liked being admired.

I was important.

I was chosen by him.

More than that, he loved me. He was absolutely committed to my well being. He cared about and for me. But something was missing in our relationship.

He loved everyone.

It was different from the kind of love between friends. The Greeks called that love "Philios".

Or between a man and a woman. The Greeks called that "Eros".

It was a pure kind of love I had never known anything about before, let alone experienced.

Later I learned the Greeks called it "agape" - god love.

He liked having me around. He loved all of us. But he loved me best. More than the rest. Oh he never said so. I could tell. I was his very special friend. I liked that.

Well, at least that is what I kept telling myself.

As time went on and I saw more and more, I found it harder and harder to believe myself. But I never gave up referring to myself as the one he loved best.

I wanted to think I was more special than anyone else in the group. I was always there with him at special times. Like the healing of Jairus' daughter. Like the time when he took us up the mountain and we saw him standing with Elijah and Moses. That was exciting.

Well, Peter and James got to go too. None of the rest.

The time came when he straightened out my thinking.

James and Peter and I got into an argument once, about which of us was the greatest of his apostles. I was sure it was me.

Jesus had a disturbing way of letting us know that he didn't like our ideas or attitudes. He could always straighten out our thinking.

He called us over and said "He who would be first, must be last!" Then he cuddled a little boy next to him and said "You see this child? Whoever receives this child receives me!"

I didn't need to ask what he was telling us with that one. Children were the lowest on the scale of important people in our society. They were somewhere just above the lepers and well below the women.

People's places in society were measured by the power they had.

Wealth!

Position within the right religious parties!

Land ownership!

These were the things that status was measured by. The aristocrats, priests, land owners, craftsmen, then day workers were all given their own level of status. Slaves had the status of their owners, because they represented their owners in the scheme of things.

These were, of course, all men.

Women had very little power so they had very little status. Without a man in their lives - a father or husband - they had no status.

Children had no power at all, but they did have some potential for power. So they had no status at all, but the potential for status. They were the lowest except for lepers.

Lepers had nothing but open weeping sores, and they would never have anything but open weeping sores.

To place himself with a child and tell us if we received such a child we received him was an enormous statement of humility.

This statement of humility, by expressing his unity with that child, was as strong as Jesus could make. He shamed our ambition and sense of self importance.

Jesus always had a habit of accepting sinners, women, lepers, slaves, People of the Land and especially children just as though they were as good as everyone else.

It was his talk about respecting all human beings as being special that led my father to give all three of his slaves freedom. They continued to stay with him and serve him. They were truly servants then - receiving an income and able to come and go as they pleased.

He never condemned us or even argued for us to do that. He helped us look at life and people differently. So that became the only right thing to do.

But now he was identifying with children.

I was stubborn and self centered. I still didn't really get the point until I talked James into something that made fools out of us. We went to Jesus and asked him, when he came into his kingdom, to have one of us on his right hand and the other on his left. We wanted the places of honor, so that we could share in the prestige of the King, the Lord of All.

We wanted to be in the important places.

I wanted to prove he loved me best and thought he would do that for me because he loved me.

"You don't know what you are asking." he said. "Can you drink the same cup I drink?" He just stared at me as if I didn't have the slightest clue as to what I was saying when I told him I could. Then he just said that wasn't up to him to give and turned away.

The rest of the apostles were pretty angry with us. They began to tell us what they thought of our idea when Jesus interrupted the whole thing and explained something to us.

Again!

The rest of the world counted things different than Jesus did. To have power over others and have them serve you was what everyone else thought was important.

Not Jesus.

To serve others and love them - that is what is important and what gained a place of high regard.

This started me to think a lot.

I had been doing things all wrong.

Despite all the things Jesus had done for me and the gifts of the Holy Spirit with which he had endowed me, I still didn't have things straight. Jairus and his family and the sickly old woman loved him as much as he loved them.

Ah ha!

I was always looking for what Jesus could do for me. I was basking in the warmth of his love. He always was doing something for me. Caring for me.

As I thought about it, the only person who ever did anything for Jesus was Mary of Magdala.

Well, I guess there were a couple of women: Mary and Martha, Lazarus sisters, and Mary of Samaria who broke her tear jars on his feet.

But that was what women are supposed to do, serve the men. Could it be that the women understood something we men had missed?

Was there a joy to serving that was its own reward?

I was always looking for what I could get. I was living a life that was based upon an idea that just didn't belong with Jesus. It wasn't what he taught or did. It wasn't what he wanted of us. It wasn't what God made us to be.

Life was different for me from then on. I finally got the point, much later than I should have!

The focus of life was no longer on being loved, but on loving.

I committed myself - an act of will - to the well-being of Jesus no matter what it cost me.

My relationship to Jesus grew in ways of which I never dreamed.

I loved him and life got better.

Little things I kept worrying about became very unimportant.

I didn't get my feelings hurt anymore.

I wasn't anxious about having things done my way anymore.

My feeling of importance had nothing to do with who admired me or where I sat.

It had everything to do with who and whose I was. It was about how positively I effected the people whose lives I touched.

After a time, what I wanted didn't really matter.

When I began to love Jesus, as he had loved me, nothing, except what I could do to express that love, mattered.

I began to love others as well as or better than I loved myself. The ancient Shema came alive for me.

It meant accepting others in their inferiority and imperfections,

without judgement,

without trying to change them before loving them!

It meant loving first, just the way they were!

It meant giving undeserved love as a product of who I am, instead of because of who they are or how lovable they are!

I discovered that the only person I have a right to require anything of is me. Trying to change the behavior of other people to please me is a terrible sin!

Ernie Bein

When we were gathered in the upper room, I was satisfied to be next to him. I really didn't mind that Judas was in the place of honor. I didn't understand how he rated, but I didn't need to.

Everything was clear later.

I finally learned that loving is more important than being loved. We are created to be loving - all of our unhappiness, our self inflicted pain, our self centered distress, is because we don't love.

So let us love one another; for love is of God, and he who loves is born of God and knows God. He who does not love does not know God; for God is love.

In this the love of God was made manifest among us, that God sent his only Son into the world, that we might live through him.

Dear friends, if God so loved us, we also ought to love one another.

No man has ever seen God; if we love one another, God abides in us and his love is perfected in us.

Chapter Five

Thomas The Twin

THE WITNESS:

Thomas was a simple and practical man. He was used to working with his hands and understood reality in pragmatic terms. He was not the brightest of the disciples. He certainly was not dumb. He had common sense and understanding that Judas, the very brightest of them all, lacked. He, at times, seemed a pessimist. That partially came from his pragmatic understanding of life. He was staunchly loyal, courageous, candid, humble, and hard working. He worked with his hands fixing things that were broken and making things people wanted and needed. Mostly he created out of iron or brass, sometimes combining these two materials with wood. He ran his business simply with a verbal agreement and the nod of the head. He was known to be fiercely honest in his business; which had gained the admiration of most and inspired clandestine attempts to swindle him by a few. He was a devout Jew and an elder in his Synagogue. A humble and common man, he was devoid of sophistication and fancy ideas. He was not easily influenced by extravagant claims. He accepted what he had experienced as truth. He was slow to accepted things without consideration and testing, all of which took time. Once he had come to understand truth he was tenaciously loyal to it. He neither accepted nor gave up his beliefs easily. He was capable of simple, but profound insight and staunchly loyal faith.

THE TESTIMONY:

I am just ordinary.

An ordinary guy.

Ernie Bein

I am an ordinary guy who somehow got to be a part of the most un - ordinary thing that has ever happened.

I am a man who has worked with his hands. I know how to shape a piece of brass or iron and make it into something useful.

I know how to take something that was not working right and make it work again.

Make it useful again.

If you can't use it, work with it, sit on it or eat with it, what good is it?

I know how to make the practical, necessary things of life that we use every day.

Or how to make them work when they were broken.

Jesus knows how to take a human life and make it into something useful.

He can fix what is broken in a person.

He cares about people and does things or teaches things that made a difference in their lives.

He is as practical as any man I ever met.

That's what I found so special about him.

I am not an expert on what the Law and Prophets tell us.

I don't know anything about all those things Judas and Matthew and Peter used to talk about.

Picking corn and eating it on the Sabbath when you are hungry makes good sense to me.

I can not understand why the Law of God would punish a man for eating when he was hungry. No matter what day it was.

Healing a man on the Sabbath and giving him two good legs to walk on seems to me like the right thing to do.

I just don't understand what all the arguing was about.

I could not imagine what would glorify God more than fixing a broken man so he was whole again, like God wanted him to be.

I don't understand laws that make life harder than it already is.

I don't want to understand politics!

What I did understand was that Jesus made me and a lot of other people feel like we are worth something.

Don't misunderstand what I mean by that.

I have never been in trouble.

I never knowingly sinned against God or my fellow man.

I was always respectable.

I never owed anyone anything.

I have always worked hard and done pretty good.

I have been a respected man in my part of Galilee.

I have worshipped in the Synagogue and paid my tithe.

I was an elder and was esteemed by my friends and neighbors who worshipped with me.

Ernie Bein

I have treated others fairly.

I have nothing to be ashamed of in my life.

I have never sought after evil.

I never thought that I was worthless.

But there is more than just not being ashamed.

There is more to life than not being worthless.

There is being worthwhile.

There is being a positive influence in a disheartened and chaotic world.

There is making a difference in the world in which you live.

I have come to understand that I can make a difference in this world.

That I might be of some special use to God and my brothers and sisters.

That is special stuff!

That is important stuff!

That is practical, day to day living kind of stuff that made life work better.

That is the kind of stuff Jesus taught us about. That is the kind of stuff Jesus taught us how to do.

Not that I understood everything he taught.

He said a lot of special things.

THE SHADOW DANCERS

Some of them were more than I could understand.

When he was talking about leaving us and about how we knew where he was going, I felt like he was talking in riddles.

So I asked a lot of questions.

Even his answers didn't always help.

Not at the time they didn't.

But now I understand.

Jesus talked in stories and I didn't always get the point.

I need people to just come right out and say what they are saying.

So I had a hard time with storytelling.

But he made me feel good about being with him anyway.

It wasn't what he said that really taught me the most.

It was what he did.

I'm not talking about the things he did like walking on water.

That got the attention of the disciples.

We all watched with open mouths.

But no.

That really didn't impress me.

Oh, I guess I was a little impressed that he could do it.

But it didn't mean anything.

No one was better off because of it.

That didn't fix anything.

How often do you need to trot across the lake to get to the other side.

We got boats for that.

Calming the storm was a little better.

That was a crowd pleaser, all right.

Sometimes stopping a storm can be very useful.

But that still isn't what really made me think.

What really counted for something was feeding all those people on the mountain side.

They were there and they were hungry and it made sense to feed them.

He sure impressed me then!

We were gathered on the hillside and it was past the meal time.

The guys were getting a little nervous.

We had families with children and women and it was a hot day sucking the energy out of everyone.

Hunger was a real companion to that crowd that day.

Most of those people seldom had all they wanted to eat.

They lived day to day on gruel and water.

What he was saying was so important and just to be close to him was so good that no one wanted to leave.

So they all just stayed and stayed.

It got late.

We traveled on a very low budget.

We always seemed to have all we needed, but never any extra.

Jesus kept telling us that if we trusted him we would never lack what we needed.

We never did.

When Judas and Peter started talking about what to do with this hungry crowd we all got a little nervous.

We didn't have the funds to buy enough food for all of them.

We didn't have the wagons to bring it back, if we did have the money.

We were in sight of several cities around the shore of the Sea.

There was Capernaum to the north.

There was Magdala just off the coast on the south west side.

There was Tiberias on the south and Gerasa on the north east.

But getting there and back was a task that did not seem practical.

I just didn't see how it was possible for us to do anything.

Ernie Bein

So I thought our suggestion was good. It seemed to make sense.

"Master, send the folks into town so they can get some food."

It was a practical thing, you see.

In this heat and out on the hillside for hours they needed sustenance to keep from getting sick.

Especially the children.

Then the little lesson time for us.

I hated it when he turned things around on us and pushed us to do things that didn't seem reasonable.

What have you got?

Nothing.

What have you got!

Well, some boy has some fish and bread. But just a little.

Bring it here.

What for?

You are going feed these people! Bring it here!

Awh Jesus! We can't do that!

Bring it here! Do what you can do. I'll take care of the rest!

Who would have believed?

Who knew?

He did.

Jesus knew!

We should have!

Just do what you can do and trust Jesus to do the rest.

What a lesson I learned!

What a very important lesson!

See what I mean about what he did teaching me so much.

If you can't be taught by a thing like that you can't be taught.

That was important stuff.

The power of God meeting the needs of people is an awesome thing to see.

I was there and I know just how wonderful it was.

Not because he did some trick of magic.

Human need was touched by the hand of God.

I have never been a very emotional man.

But I got chills up my back when I thought about it.

That kind of stuff made sense.

All those folks he healed!

Now that really made sense.

Helpless, hopeless folks suddenly became able to do for themselves.

People who were a burden to someone, or suffering incomplete lives because of physical or mental problems were set free to be all they could be.

People captured by the evil one freed of his power.

Like Mary of Magdala. What a case she was.

Nasty!

She invented mean!

What a difference he made by just setting her free.

That was practical and sensible.

How did He do it?

I didn't know.

I didn't care!

It seemed to me a waste of time trying to explain why and how.

He did it.

Peoples lives were better because he did.

I can never know or understand everything, so why bother worrying about what does not matter.

He did it.

That matters.

I didn't care how!

I had more important things to care about.

What I did care about was that there were people who had become whole - who were useful - who did not ache when they tried to move - who could live happy healthy lives.

That was important stuff.

Real stuff.

And I was there and a part of it.

Life was more important that I ever thought it could be.

Trouble came.

Actually, trouble started to follow us.

No matter how many lives were changed for the better, or how good he was; or how right he was about what he said; or how kind and loving and generous he was; there were always men who stood back waiting.

Waiting because he was different and they couldn't admit they were wrong and he was right.

Waiting because he threatened their position or authority or belief system.

They were waiting for a chance to get him.

He didn't stick to the party line.

He didn't do what all the other Pharisees did.

He went past them to a new level of love.

They didn't understand that.

They didn't approve of that.

They didn't like that.

The aristocrats and Romans didn't like anyone who was a leader of any consequence.

They were afraid of the people.

The sheer numbers of people could be a decided threat to their well being if the right leader organized them and set them upon those who controlled the nation.

But the people were not a danger without a leader.

So they kept their eyes on emerging leaders and squashed them if they got too big.

He knew it.

He knew it all, but did what he needed to do without letting them influence who or what he was.

He refused to protect himself.

He refused to avoid them; to go where they had no power.

What he did wasn't sensible.

He went right into Jerusalem, faced them down at the Temple and caused all sorts of stir.

"Asking for trouble!" I called it.

THE SHADOW DANCERS

I knew we were in trouble as soon as he turned his face to Jerusalem. I did not need to be a prophet to understand what was going to happen once we got to Jerusalem.

Common sense was all anyone needed to figure that out.

I really thought we would all die.

What else could I do but go with him?

I had to follow him wherever he went.

How we all escaped tests reason.

We should all have been sweep up and killed when he was.

Somehow, something got us clear - moved us out of harm's way when we had to be.

I didn't understand it then.

I might understand it now.

God's hand was upon us and he needed us to carry the Word.

So we survived despite the reasonable idea that we couldn't.

Just when I would get comfortable with a practical point of view and satisfied I had it right, Jesus would teach me something new again.

That was and is how it is with Jesus.

The night they came for him was terrible.

The women screamed.

Peter acted like a fool.

Ernie Bein

Judas was kissing him at the same time he was signaling to the temple guards and soldiers to take him.

That made no sense!

Jesus offered no resistance.

He went with them without a word.

The next few days were hard.

We pretty much hid.

I did sneak around to get a peek at him whenever I could.

When I did see him I wished I hadn't.

There wasn't much left of his back when they finished with the whip.

Scourging was not an uncommon method of punishment.

There were several kinds of scourging.

The least brutal was done with a wooden rod and left bruises in varied degrees of severity according to how long and how hard a person was beaten.

Roman scourging, "flagellum", was the worst and was meant as a substitute for crucifixion.

It was done with a multi - tail whip with pieces of sharp steel tied to the ends of the lashes.

Each stroke of the executioner left eighty one slashes on a man's back.

Thirty nine lashes were the absolute maximum a human being could stand without dying.

Forty killed you.

Sometimes fewer killed weaker or older men.

Thirty nine crippled you for the rest of your life.

All the muscle was torn from a man's back and shoulders and left in a sickening pile of gore around his feet on the ground.

He could not lift his arms.

They would just dangle forward.

He was a made a cripple for life, left to beg at the gate for alms.

It was very practical, you see.

A man could never bear arms or lead and army in such a crippled condition.

He also was a gruesome living reminder of what happened to anyone who encountered the anger of Roman.

In one way it made more sense to scourge than to crucify.

A Crucifixion ended in death and after a few days the body had been eaten by the vultures and was gone.

It was over, then, you see.

Scourging left a living sign of horror, a cripple at the city gates begging for alms.

Such a lesson was a more lasting one.

Ernie Bein

His back was gone.

His ribs showed white out of the bloody gore that used to be his back.

The thorns in his scalp made more blood run down in his eyes.

They laid the cross on his back and wrapped and tied his arms around it, making him grab it with what little strength was left in those hands.

Those strong hands.

Now bloody and trembling with pain.

Those gentle caring hands that held children and touched the sick and dead with miraculous power to heal.

Those hands that gestured when he laughed and lovingly touched a friends shoulder.

That trembled now with pain.

I vomited and cried.

By the time they nailed him to the wood he was already nearly dead.

It was strange.

He should not have survived the nailing and hanging.

He lasted a lot longer than he should have lasted.

It was like he wasn't going to die until he was ready to die. He seemed to have some things to say and do first.

When it was over I didn't feel free to leave the city.

I was scared.

I thought I might be next.

I stayed in hiding and planned to leave a few days after the "official" Passover.

The crowds on the roads would be the biggest then.

You see, Jesus, other Pharisees, the Essenes and some others celebrated the Passover according to our ancient Jewish lunar calendar.

The Sadducees, who were in control of the country and Temple, had, as a part of their political capitulation, run the nation and the Temple according to the Roman solar calendar.

So we celebrated the Passover several days before the "official" Passover.

The majority of the people celebrated when the Sadducees said so.

So the biggest crowds would gather at the "official" time.

Most of us stayed together around that upstairs room.

Judas was dead now too, so no one knew about that room except us and it was safe.

I returned there one night to some foolish stories.

The women, especially Mary of Magdala, claimed they had seen him.

Then all of them went crazy.

He had been there with them, they said.

Walked right through the door, they said.

(Muffles a laugh)

Through the door!

They said. (Disgustedly)

It was bad enough when the women got foolish, seeing what they wanted to see and believing what they wanted to believe.

But they all were doing it.

Not a sensible person in the bunch.

If they said he was still alive in our hearts I would have agreed.

If they said his spirit was with us forever, I would had have no argument.

If they said they still felt his love. Great!

If they said what he taught and what he did would live in this world forever, I would have affirmed that too.

But to say he was alive again didn't make sense.

I was disgusted with their inability to accept reality.

It just didn't make sense.

It wasn't real.

That isn't how things happen.

This isn't a hundred years ago or a thousand.

We are smarter than all of that now.

We understand about life and death.

The community may survive - the remnant left behind when others die.

But dead people are dead and that is the end of that.

They need to stop living with old superstitions and live in the present day.

They had killed him.

That was real!

I missed Him and grieved for him.

That was real!

I had curled up in the corner of the night and wept silently to myself because it hurt me so deeply.

I missed him so.

That was a reality I could not escape with some silly stories.

I was scared of what might still happen to me.

That was real!

In the middle of all that reality there was no place for silly dreams about him being alive again.

I couldn't understand why they wouldn't face reality and get on with life.

I just wanted them to leave him alone and let him be.

He was dead and that was that.

I wished they would let me alone and let me be.

Not try to get me to believe their silly talk.

Talk was talk and life was life and you couldn't change life by wishing.

That was reality - I thought.

I thought.

I was wrong.

I found out reality is not always what we think it is.

There is a reality beyond brass and iron.

Beyond death?

Yes!

There is a reality beyond even death.

I have faced that reality.

I have seen with my own eyes.

I have heard with my own ears.

I am an **ordinary** man.

I am not given to hysteria.

I am an **ordinary, practical man**!

Yet, I have been face to face with the most un - ordinary event - no - the most extraordinary event that has ever happened.

I've seen Jesus who was dead and isn't dead anymore.

Jesus, who I saw mutilated by the whip and hung upon a cross until he was dead - DEAD - and now he is alive and whole.

He lives.

Now!

He is alive!

He is alive now and forever!

He, who is my Lord, is alive.

He, who is my God is alive.

Forever!

Grass grows, withers and dies. It is gone.

Or so it seems.

Some say that is how people are.

They say that all the things we learn, all that we experience, all that we are, comes to a stone wall at death and stops forever.

Like grass, we grow, flourish, then wither and die and are gone.

Grass comes back after the rains.

It greens up and lives again.

What has died is only the part that shows.

Ernie Bein

The roots are still there and sprout new blades.

That makes a lot of sense to me about how life in this world is.

Jesus showed us that life does not slam into a stone wall called death.

Jesus has proved that isn't so.

This life is just a beginning.

All that we are is not lost, but lives on.

Why do I follow a dead man?

Because he lives!

And so do I!

That sure makes good sense to me!

Chapter Six

Mary Magdalene

THE WITNESS:

Mary was the daughter of a wealthy merchant of the fortress city of Magdala. An affliction in her teenage and early adult years made her unsuitable for marriage. So she was still under the protection of her father's house. Her father had personally suffered with her behavior problems and was overjoyed at the difference Jesus has made in her life. She had followed Jesus since she was delivered by him, and has used her resources to support him and his followers. Her wealth came from her father who, motivated by his daughter's new life, was generous to Jesus ministry. She was close to Jesus and was the only one around him who, from the beginning, loved him without expectations. While others had looked at what Jesus could do for them, she had looked for what she could do for Jesus. Mary loved Jesus, but was not his lover. She loved him with the same unselfish love with which he loved her. In that time and place, only a woman could have had the insight and skill to have ministered to Jesus as he needed ministering unto. A key and necessary part of the disciples who followed Jesus, Mary had a very special place. There was a strong difference between what Mary used to be and what she became. A gracious, kind, compassionate, loving and even genteel lady.

THE TESTIMONY:

I wasn't always like that, out of control and hopeless.

When I was a child I was happy and loved.

I had three older brothers who treated me as though I were a little princess.

I had parents who loved me deeply.

My father was a successful business man in a city on the Roman Road that connected Egypt to Antioch, called Magdala.

Magdala was a very sophisticated place to grow up.

It was a fortress city.

Each Roman region had such a place for the Roman army to retreat into in the event of a war.

A walled city was populated by different people than open cities like Tibereas or Capernaum. We Jews were fewer the four in every one hundred people in Magdala.

Where other cities on the Roman Road only saw people of different nations pass through, we lived with them.

There was more commerce than agricultural.

It was an exciting place to live as a child and an alluring one when I was an adolescent.

I had everything I needed to be happy.

I was spoiled by indulgent parents.

I knew how pretty I was and liked people to notice.

I also knew that I was smarter than most.

I did not want people to know that.

I loved the stories of Rachel and Ruth. I loved hearing about Ruth and how she said to Naomi "Where you go I will go, where you stay I will stay, your people will be my people and your God will be my God."

I dreamed of being her when she was in the field gleaning. She was so beautiful that she captured Moab's heart the minute he saw her.

I loved, even more, hearing the story about Jacob and Rachel.

She was so beautiful that Jacob worked for Laban for fourteen years in order to marry her.

He loved her so!

I dreamed of being her and watching the handsome Jacob working with the flocks, the sweat making his body glisten in the sun.

I dreamed of her wedding night.

Not always do we marry someone we love.

Usually we learn to love someone we marry!

Our fathers, especially when they were as wealthy as mine, picked a rich man who may not have been as handsome or as passionate or as young as the boys we saw in the city.

But we - I - dreamed anyway. About love and marriage and having children - I dreamed.

Dreaming was nearly the only thing I had to do. I was taught all the things girls are supposed to learn about being a wife, mother and running a household.

I had servants to do all the real work and it was presumed I would marry a man who could provide enough servants to please me.

I was very smart and learned all my lessons well.

That didn't take much effort at all.

So dreaming is what I spent most of my time doing.

I know how to be a good Jewish mother and wife.

I learned how to teach and discipline children, how to plan and prepare meals, and run the household correctly.

I learned how to keep accounts so my husband's money was spent wisely.

I learned how to observe what children and men liked so that I could provide for their comfort.

I learned how a gentle touch on a man's shoulders or a stroke on his brow can relax and comfort a man. I had brothers to practice on.

My mother didn't teach me much of anything about sex. She said that there were some things you didn't need to be taught in order to get right.

I looked forward to the time my father would pick me a husband. I was sure I could influence him to find someone I really loved. He did dote on me, you see.

I began to get anxious to grow up to be eligible for marriage.

I was also bored.

I was inquisitive and looked for new experiences.

An Egyptian mystic showed me some of his magic and I became curious.

After I had spent much time listening to his special secrets and watching him do things that couldn't be done, he taught me some special incantations and mystical spells.

I was curious and excited.

It sounded so exciting, I rushed into some things with which I ought never to have been involved.

I was very strong willed.

I knew my parents would object.

So I never told them about what I was getting into.

They never really understood what went on in my life to change me so.

I had opened myself to spiritual things I didn't understand.

I found myself deeper and deeper under the control of some *"other"* that I did not know and could not describe.

I lost control of my life.

I lost hope for myself.

I did and said things that were offensive, even disgusting to other people.

And to myself.

Like throwing dung at the bride at a wedding.

Like screaming obscenities at people leaving the synagogue.

Like curling up in a pig pen on the feces and urine soaked mud.

Ernie Bein

I seemed to find the vilest things I could, and either did or said them.

I inflicted injury upon those I loved and myself.

I kept hearing this voice saying to me "you aren't pretty - that is an ugly face - it should be beaten until it is gone". I tried to smash my face with a stone. My father stopped me and restrained me until I stopped trying.

Some times I would just roll around the floor and scream.

It was like someone else was in control!

A lot of other someones.

I never understood why I did those things.

I reached marrying age, but no one wanted me, even though I was considered very pretty (despite my efforts to change that) and had been brought up to be a good wife.

I was damaged goods, put aside, out of the way, because I was more of a problem than a wife should be.

No one wanted to take home such a nasty person as was I.

I saw the pain in my father's eyes.

I heard the anguish in my mother's voice.

I watched the sadness eat at my brothers.

But I was powerless to change. I was too weak to overcome the evil that consumed me.

After a time, I didn't try anymore. I had a snarl for everyone and a vicious word for those who loved me most.

I didn't know who or what I was.

It was as if I were a lot of different persons all fighting to control each other.

I was desperate.

Father would have been glad to have kept me hidden.

I refused to stay hidden.

I would sneak out.

I would escape the servants who were put with me to keep me out of sight.

I wanted people to see how degraded I had become.

I was a public embarrassment.

I wanted to be a public embarrassment.

Then father heard of this man who had power over evil.

He took me to see the man at Capernaum and begged for him to use his power.

He delivered me.

He commanded the evil in me to leave and it did.

Only one who has been imprisoned can know what it means to be set free.

I didn't know I was imprisoned until I was freed.

I was freed by Jesus.

Set free to be who I am and to chose how I should act and talk.

Free to be me.

The real me.

But that isn't all.

He taught me.

He taught me that only Satan seeks to control.

He taught me God allows us to choose or not to choose to do his will.

He taught me that God loves us so much he refuses to control us.

He frees us to choose good or evil.

He taught all of us.

He taught us that we must be in control of our own lives, but must never try to control others.

He taught us that we become like Satan when we manipulate others to do and be what we choose.

He taught us that to love is the most important thing in life.

To love the way he loved was unconditional and other centered, instead of self centered.

He taught me how to do that.

I listened to his words and watched what he did.

I learned from him.

I learned to love.

He showed me such deep, unconditional love.

I learned to love him in a way that others did not understand.

It made me angry that no one else seemed to care about how he felt. Or notice how tired he got.

All any of them seemed to care about was what he could do for **them.**

They were always crying out for what they wanted:

"Heal me, Jesus!",

"Save me, Jesus!",

"Forgive Me, Jesus!",

"Feed me, Jesus!",

"Give me a place of honor, Jesus!",

"Teach me, Jesus!",

"Love me, Jesus!"

Never did any of them cry out "We love you, Jesus!"

It seemed so strange to me that no one else noticed that he needed love too.

With my father's permission, I followed Jesus.

I was always discrete, as a woman should be. I stayed apart from the men with a few other women.

It was amazing to us that he never treated us like other men did.

We had all been raised to be completely subservient to men.

All men!

We were not mistreated by men.

Actually, we were, more often than not, treated gently and with respect by men.

We were, however, just sort of kept in our place.

He seemed to lift us on to higher ground, standing on the same level with men.

We didn't always know how to handle that.

The men **never** knew how to handle it.

We (father and I) used my father's money to support what Jesus was doing.

Actually, all of the women had a financial source from husbands and fathers to contribute to the support of Jesus minstry.

Jesus had done very well as a carpenter.

Just as the Johns and the Zebedees had done well as fishermen.

Thomas had done well as an artisan and so on.

However, all of their personal wealth was not sufficient to provide for families back home and the one hundred or so disciples who traveled with us.

Any itinerant teacher needed financial support. We could not be sent out two by two to heal and teach. We, the women, served in other ways, including financially.

I had a special place in his life.

It wasn't the kind of romantic thing I dreamed about as a girl.

I learned to minister to him. I did all the little things a woman can do to make him comfortable: good food, cool water for his brow or feet, a warm smile, a grateful hug, or an attentive ear when he just needed to tell someone about his joys, frustration or fears.

Sometimes at night I would just sit with his head in my lap and we would talk. I would stroke his face with my finger tips - very lightly. I would just sort of whisper my fingers across his face. It would relax him. Sometimes he would fall asleep that way.

Sometimes he would let me curl up in his arms and he would hold me when I was nervous or frightened.

He knew I loved him, but we never spoke of it.

I knew that I could never be his wife, but after learning to know him, I knew I could never marry another and be happy. No other man could ever measure up to him.

These were the happiest and saddest days of my life.

We laughed a lot. Jesus was fun to be around. He kept everyone smiling much of the time.

That line about having a log in your eye when you are trying to take a speck out of another's eye had people giggling for days. We all shared some very happy times.

There were times when I cried for him.

Ernie Bein

I cried for the way they all pulled at him.

I cried for the way they wore him out.

I cried at the weariness I saw in his face.

I would cry over the evil I saw that others wanted to do to him.

I cried over the danger I sensed for him.

I cried for those who refused to see who and whose he was.

I cried a lot.

But mostly silently and to myself.

Yet he knew when I was crying.

He always knew why.

He would just smile and say my name.

I could have my back turned and he would say my name that special way he had of saying it and I knew it was him.

I always felt safe then.

All the fears and sadness flew away when he said my name.

Sometimes he would just smile and say my name as if to ask "Why are you crying while I am giving you all this love?"

I would always smile through my tears and stop.

Sometimes, when I was crying a little more than silently he would say "It shouldn't rain while the sun shines, Mary."

THE SHADOW DANCERS

I would remember, then, that as long as I had him near, no one could steal my joy.

I didn't know how much crying I would do.

I was afraid for Him when we entered Jerusalem.

My fear grew like grass during the spring rains.

Soon it was a hot ball in my stomach.

The terror became hideous for me.

I was never afraid of what anyone might do to me.

I was in trembling fits over what I became sure they were going to do to him.

That night in the garden, when we heard the East Gate creek on its hinges as they opened it, I wanted to cry out, "Run Jesus, run before they get here." By the time they came down the hill in front of the gate and came back up this side he could have been over the crest of the hill and lost in the dark.

He didn't move.

We just watched the torches come toward us, down the hill in front of the wall of the city and climb up to us.

Not all of us watched. Peter, James and John had fallen asleep under some olive trees.

He prayed and waited for them.

Then we could see the faces of the men with the torches.

He stood up, called the Zebedees and Peter and went to meet the group led by Judas as though he were greeting guests of honor.

Ernie Bein

I cried as they took him.

I cried as my heart broke in the next days.

I cried when they mocked him.

I cried when they beat him.

I cried when they shredded his back with the whip.

I cried when they nailed him.

I cried when he died.

I cried that night and the next day and night. I cried because there had been nothing I could do for him. Because he suffered terribly. Because he was dead and it wasn't fair.

But mostly I cried because the love of my life was dead and I missed him so.

I would never be able to curl up in his arms and be comforted again.

I could never whisper my fingers on his face again.

I wanted him back. I knew I would never see him again.

I was still crying when we went to the tomb to prepare his body.

It was the last thing I could do for Him.

Nicodemus had left a great quantity of Myrrh and Aloe in the cave with his body for the preparation.

I had not been able to do anything until the first day of the week because of the Sabbath.

So I went very early to care for his body.

But it was gone!

The stone was rolled back up the slid and a rock held it in place at the top of the trough away from the cave entrance.

The cave was empty!

I ran and got Peter and John.

Men!

All they did was look in and say "Yes, Mary it is gone. It really is. The body most definitely is gone."

Then they left.

I wanted them to find it.

I wanted them to put it back so I could take care of it.

But they left.

It wasn't fair.

My dear Jesus had been tortured and killed.

I was being robbed of his presence in my life.

Now I couldn't even prepare his body the way it ought to be for the tomb.

Then I really cried.

I thought I had used up all my tears and none were left.

Ernie Bein

But I let loose a torrent of tears.

A flood flowed from my eyes.

There was nothing silent about my crying now.

I howled like bitten dog.

Through the tears I saw a brilliant light coming from the tomb.

My sobs slowed, but didn't stop.

I looked back into the tomb again, and was nearly blinded by the brilliance of two persons sitting there on the shelf where he had been.

"Why are you crying?" they asked.

I thought "What a dumb question!", but I told them anyway.

Then I sensed some one behind me and turned.

I saw a man standing with his back to the morning sun.

I was blinded by the sun, so I assumed he was the gardener

I shouted at him "If you have carried him away, tell me where you have laid him and I will take him away and care for him."

Or something like that.

I was blubbering so much I am not sure exactly what I said.

I cried louder and harder than ever before.

Then he spoke my name!.

It was as if he had just said "It shouldn't rain when the sun shines, Mary."

He spoke my name as only he could.

I smiled through my tears and stopped crying.

I rushed to him, but he wouldn't let me hold him.

My heart pounded and I couldn't catch my breath.

My aching eyes wanted to cry again, but now in delirious joy.

My Jesus was alive.

My sweet Jesus was alive!

I didn't understand how.

I didn't even wonder about why.

Jesus was alive!

Jesus is alive!

I knew I will never be alone again.

Or frightened again.

Or worried about the rest of my life.

Or worried about dying.

Or anything again.

Ever!

"Why me?" I wondered.

Peter and John had just been here.

Why did he wait to show himself just to me?

Was it because, of all of them, I was the only one who loved him.

Who truly loved him, the way he loved me.

Was I as special to him as he was to me?

I have held that hope in my heart.

I did as he told me to do and went back and told them what I had seen.

I told them I had just seen Jesus.

They really didn't understand or believe me until later when he came to them.

That was alright.

I really didn't care. They could believe me or not.

Jesus is alive.

Nothing in this world is strong enough to destroy him.

He has been with me for every minute since then.

He is alive and he chose me to be the first to know.

I may not ever cry again!

Chapter Seven

Nicodemas

THE WITNESS:

He was a very wealthy, a very bright, and a very old teacher. A member of the Sanhedrin, he carried a lot of influence. He was a Pharisee, so he had strong sense of right and wrong. Pharisees had developed a list of do's and don'ts in addition to the Law to fine tune everyday life for every person. All persons were to live righteous lives, not just a few holy men. Pharisees themselves expected more of themselves and each other than they did of the common man. They emphasized a righteous daily life as more important than the rites and rituals performed in worship. He believed in a personal eternal life, (salvation for the person as opposed to only salvation of the nation through the remnant). He was aware of his social position as well as his influence upon the spiritual condition of many devout persons. He carried that burden carefully and was therefore appropriately cautious. He had to be sure before openly acknowledging Jesus as the Messiah, although he was convinced that it was true. Nicodemus was a strong and devout man who had too much to lose for himself and the many people who looked to him for guidance. He was, therefore, reluctant to risk open support of Jesus. He was waiting to make absolutely sure. Yet his fellow members of the Sanhedrin suspected his position and found it necessary to avoid trying to condemn Jesus in his presence.

THE TESTIMONY:

I had watched him grow up.

I watched him grow in body, mind and spirit.

Once I had met him, I could never forget him.

Ernie Bein

It was many years ago.

He came to the temple and I was teaching.

He was only a boy, not yet, but almost, a man.

Yet his questions amazed us.

He was anxious to learn.

His questions gave away an insight that needed nurturing.

He knew his Hebrew very well, and at times asked us theological questions in the holy tongue.

Through the years I have seen him a few times.

He was frequent at the holy feasts and Passover.

He was always so special.

Those occasional encounters burned into my memory the **image of one chosen by God.**

He had grown in favor with God and man.

I was pleased, but not surprised when he became one of us.

He learned his father's trade. As a craftsman he was free to study and then to teach as a Pharisee did.

We all have crafts to support ourselves. This gave us both an independence and a financial resource to be about our real work, teaching the word of God to the people of God.

Once committed to this life few of us marry.

THE SHADOW DANCERS

We seldom had time for a wife and children. Our lives were too full of God's work. Our love was for the people who needed to grow in God's ways so they could have full and joyous lives.

Most larger towns and all cities in the area had Synagogues.

As our people were moved to other parts of the world some of us would always make sure we were there too.

We would organize Synagogues and teach the people. Our nation survived even after the fall of Jerusalem because we were there with the people teaching them the tradition and Law and explaining the Prophets.

That is what we did.

We were the teachers - the Rabbis - who taught the people and called them to righteousness.

Actually there were two kinds of Pharisees.

There were the Scribes who were intensely involved in understanding every detail and inference of the Law. They were the consultants, persons to whom we could go to get a better understanding of some detail of the rules by which we lived.

Most of us were teachers - Rabbis - who taught the people and led them to righteousness.

We loved the people.

The Priests cared little for the people.

As long as they got their tithes and the people celebrated the temple high holy days with sacrifices, the priests didn't care what else happened.

The Priests were, as a group, mechanically religious.

There was a lack of compassionate concern for the well being of the people.

The nation is all they worried about.

The people they didn't worry about.

If a person did the right mechanical things, had sacrificed enough, had brought enough grain offerings and learned to doven while praying, then that person was righteous.

According to the Priests they were righteous.

They didn't care about what they did in their everyday life.

As a matter of fact, many of the Priests didn't care what they themselves did in their everyday lives.

We believed that God expected us to be righteous everyday!

I don't mean to say that all Priests were hypocrites and all Pharisees holy!

That wasn't true.

There were some righteous men and good men among the Priests.

There were some self righteous snobs among the Pharisees.

Some of us got so caught up in the Law we forgot about the people.

Jesus sure told us about it when he saw that among us.

We knew what the Law and Prophets taught.

We didn't always do it.

I don't mean to speak triflingly about dovening either.

I love to celebrate the worship of God.

I am thrilled when the scrolls are read.

I enjoyed sitting in the Moses Seat and teaching.

But what I love best is the prayer time.

When a Synagogue full of devout men who knew their prayer Hebrew perfectly, stood shoulder to shoulder in line after line reciting their prayers and dovening in perfect time to the rhythm of the Hebrew words, it was a marvelous act of adoration I know God loved.

One who dovened well seemed to have a string from his chin and through his hands to his knees so that when he stood, head bowed, hands together in front of his chest and he began to doven it looked like someone was pulling the string out the back of his knees so his head, hands and knees moved toward each other in perfect symmetry.

We lived mostly throughout the country.

Very few of us lived in Jerusalem.

Those of us that did were in pretty constant debate with the Sadducees who dominated the nation and the Sanhedrin.

Jesus had moved from Nazareth and had been teaching in Capernaum for several years.

He seemed to feel uncomfortable with the way things were in Jerusalem and at the temple.

He made his regular pilgrimages for the Holy Days, but didn't seem satisfied with what he saw there.

Ernie Bein

There was a growing righteousness within him we all came to admire.

That is why I was so surprised to see him with The Baptizer at the Ford of Bethbara.

Why would he need to answer a call to repentance?

He had lived and was living a righteous life.

He was already sitting in the Moses Seat of the Synagogue.

Was he submitting himself as a disciple to that crude Essene in animal skins?

That was a needless fear.

It became clear when he came down out of the wilderness.

No human mind would control or direct him.

His teaching always had the ring of truth.

When he spoke, it seemed to fit all that I knew of the Lord.

I was just as enthralled as the People of the Land who crowded hillside and shorelines to hear him.

I always came away with a deeper joy in the Lord after hearing him teach.

Yet there were ways in which he did not fit our code of ethics.

He did and said things that were not what we had taught him.

Things he did - people he ate with - places he went - just were not what a good Pharisee was supposed to do.

THE SHADOW DANCERS

We have rules, you know.

Rules are important.

We have, over several centuries, tried to figure out what to do in every human situation and make a rule for it.

We believed that if you keep the rules - all the rules - you would be righteous in God's eyes.

He wasn't keeping all the rules.

That was a worry.

I had to be careful.

You see, I too had grown in the Lord and in the eyes of my people.

I had become highly respected.

Even the Sadducees gave me respect.

They acknowledge the wisdom of my teachings and the depth of my understandings.

I was never challenged upon my understanding of the Law.

Only Gamaliel was given respect equal to mine in the Sanhedrin and at the Temple.

When I spoke people listened.

If I insisted, others acquiesced.

Few directly opposed my opinions.

Oh, I know there are those who disagreed with me.

Ernie Bein

I had risen to a place of power and influence among my people.

My opposition was avoided, rather than challenged, in the Sanhedrin.

There were, at times, meetings held that I didn't know about, until later. Something was always done I didn't approve of happening at those meetings.

My life was my witness.

I had worked hard at being good.

I knew how to be the very best person for God I could possibly be.

I **was** that person.

I was secure in the knowledge that I was a good man.

I was certain God would bless my goodness with eternal life.

I was certain, until I heard Jesus.

Then I began to wonder.

He taught things I had never dreamed of, yet sensed were true.

It wasn't that we ever disagreed.

It was more like he had moved past me in his spiritual understanding.

It is hard to teach something all your life, and then watch a much younger man, a man to whom you had been the very first teacher, bend and stretch all the rules and still come out sounding so right.

So I needed to know as much as he could teach me.

The critical question for me was eternal life.

Unlike the Sadducees, I found it a shallow answer to suggest that the Law and Prophets talk of immortality only in the sense of the continuation of the community of God.

Or as a remembrance of those who have contributed to the common good.

Or to live in the hearts of the people.

I believed I would be.

I believed I would be with God.

But Jesus was saying all my goodness would not get me there.

It was like having to start my life all over again.

He talked about a relationship.

A spiritual relationship.

With him.

That was a problem!

You see I was too respected to expect that my openly following Jesus would go unnoticed.

If I did that, others would do so too, not because of him, but just because I did.

That would not be acceptable.

Their relationship with him needed to be first hand.

Ernie Bein

What if it turned out I was wrong about him! I would be mocked as a foolish old man.

I would have done terrible damage to the spiritual condition of many people.

I would have given the Sadducees a chance to undermine my influence in the Sanhedrin.

Lord knows I've kept them from making a lot of unfortunate decisions.

My word has been heard in that body time and time again and the people and nation have always been better off because of it.

I was important to the well being of the people.

That was an awesome responsibility.

It was, therefore, important for me to go slowly.

To wait and see.

Not to allow emotion to over ride reason!

To make sure I would not lose out by being too quick to follow.

It was just too risky.

I spoke up for him a few times.

Once the Sanhedrin sent out the temple guards to seize him.

They returned empty handed and in awe of him and his words.

Some of us were furious.

THE SHADOW DANCERS

When I spoke up suggesting that the Law did not support hearsay and blind accusation, I was whispered about around the room.

I understand a few spoke abusively about me when I was not present.

They were reputed to have attacked my ability to reason.

Even though I was careful not to publicly follow him, the others knew.

I had to be even more careful.

When they finally had him arrested and convened the Sanhedrin they made sure I wasn't told about it.

I was absent for the trial.

I want to think I could have spared him.

But, then all that did happen would not have happened.

I guess it really had to go the way it did.

I guess there was no other way.

I just wish he had not had to go through all of that suffering.

When Joseph and I claimed his body, we had to be especially cautious.

It seemed all was lost.

It was over.

He was dead.

I thought I was wrong about him.

I still cared about him, but I was wrong.

He couldn't have been the Messiah or they wouldn't have been able to kill Him.

Not like that.

Not at all!

Then I was pleased that I had not been too hasty.

But not for long.

I soon found that I should have been quicker to stand up for him and to sit at his feet.

That was clear on that glorious morning.

He had taken the very worst the world could do to him and he won over it all.

Nothing in this world can stop the will of God or destroy us.

Hallelujah!

I had been wrong.

Very wrong.

But not about who he was.

Funny isn't it.

I had always had to be right.

I was wrong about the most important thing in my life.

I had failed to risk.

I had missed the most important opportunity of my lifetime.

Of anybody's lifetime.

Of **everybody's** lifetime.

I am so glad all that doesn't matter anymore.

I am so glad eternal life isn't decided by how good we are.

Or how right we are.

I am so grateful for forgiveness.

I am so glad that the mistakes I have made don't count.

I know now it is OK to risk.

To even be wrong sometimes.

That was a heavy burden, never being allowed to be wrong.

I'm free of that now.

Why, it's just like starting life fresh and new all over again.

Chapter Eight

Simon the Zealot

THE WITNESS:

Simon was poor. Somewhere back a generation or so his family had owned land. He was like most of the people native to the fertile crescent. Taxes had forced land sales and reduced life to drudgery. He was a member of an oppressed people. His family had been oppressed and his children would be too, if he didn't do something to change it all. He wanted war. He was an ardent revolutionary. His faith system led him to expect a deliverer in the image of Judas Maccabeaus. His life and expectations were altered significantly after he followed Christ.

THE TESTIMONY:

Life wasn't much fun.

I would get up before the sun every day. I would go to the market and wait until a steward or landowner came.

If chosen that day I would work harder than anyone else and try harder than anyone else hoping that the boss would notice and remember me the next day.

Or whenever he came back for workers again.

I seldom finished work until dark.

I would go home with my pay and give it to my wife.

THE SHADOW DANCERS

She planned for the next days food from it. Usually three days worth of food, since it wasn't usual for me to not get work for several days in a row.

I ate supper, usually a mealy gruel. The longer it had been since I worked, the more watered down the gruel was.

Maybe I would have a pomegranate.

Maybe a few grapes. Meat happened only a couple times a year.

After I ate, I went to bed.

Next morning it started all over again.

Up before the sun.

Hoping someone would hire me.

Standing erect and trying to look strong in the market.

That was to impress whoever might be looking for workers.

If you sat down, no matter how long you had been standing there, it made a bad impression.

There was always this knot in my stomach.

I was afraid!

I was afraid I wouldn't get hired.

I was afraid I would get work, and would have to work harder than a man should have to work.

I was afraid I would, some day, work myself to death. Working in the hot sun out in the fields.

I was getting old. I was nearly thirty. I couldn't work the way I once did. I knew some day soon, I would not be as hireable as I once was. So I was afraid the day would come soon I would be even worse off than I now was.

I was always afraid of what the day would bring when I stood in the market.

It was the same everyday.

Some days I didn't get work.

Many days I would not get work.

I stayed at the market all day.

Waiting.

Hoping.

Sometimes a landowner or steward would come back later in the day, because the work wasn't getting finished by the people who went out early.

Sometimes that might happen, but not very often.

The Sabbath was just another day.

You had to work if anyone would hire you.

Life wasn't very good.

It was mostly a struggle to survive.

The worst part was the way the owners or stewards would treat us when we were working, or begging for work.

Like dogs.

Like panting, vomit eating dogs.

Not men.

Not men, but animals.

To be used up until we died in our tracks.

Get as much work as they could from us for as little pay as they could get by with!

That was their goal.

They didn't care about anything, but their own interests.

Every once in awhile anger would boil up to the surface and a steward would end up found dead in the field.

Nobody ever knew who was working for him that day.

It was just a mystery.

All of us understood how it happened.

But not all of us would do it.

It wasn't smart.

We might all go for weeks without work after that. Better to let crops rot in the field than to be killed by those you hired to work those fields.

I always thought that sort of thing was foolish, but sometimes men can only take so much. Men have to be men. When men are treated like they are less than human, bad things happen.

I never killed anyone.

But I wanted to.

And began planning to.

But not the landowners.

Or the stewards.

Violence against them was misplaced.

Such violence was the product of an explosion of anger.

I was ready to carefully plan any violence I was going to do.

Nothing was gained by killing anyone who had no power to change things. Or rather, whose death would not change things.

It was time for a revolution.

There were many who agreed with me. There was a whole army of us.

There were weapons hidden in places we could get to.

There were persons who watched every Roman move in this land.

If we were treated badly by our employers, we were treated pitifully by our oppressors.

This was our land. But they treated us as though we were the strangers. It was unavoidable. Revolution had to come.

Even those, whose families had not lived in this land for centuries, were fed up with this life.

They were there on the market and fields next to us. Theirs was even a deeper anger. They had been transported into this land by the Romans and the Greeks before them.

They weren't like us.

They didn't look like us.

But they suffered like us.

They too, were ready to do something about our plight.

When men are treated like dogs they will do terrible things, sooner or later, to their tormentors.

"An eye for an eye" say the scriptures.

Well there had been a lot of eyes, and ears, and mouths, and the bodies attached to them of men that had been destroyed by those smug little foreigners.

Justice was going to be done.

"Let justice roll down like waters." said the prophet.

Well, justice is what we wanted. To punish the sins of our oppressors.

To regain our dignity.

To claim our land back.

The way to have justice was to let Roman blood flow like water. We had to eliminate every one of those greasy little foreigners.

Freedom!

We dreamed of freedom!

Ernie Bein

Our freedom!

I dreamed of our nation without a foreign army with its foot on our neck.

When all men were free to do and be whatever they wanted.

Where justice was swift and fair.

What we needed - all we needed - was a leader.

Someone like Judas Maccabeaus.

Someone to lead us into battle with the blessing and power of God upon our swords.

So that, with God's power behind us, we could slaughter every ugly Roman in our land and send back a message to Rome, as we had two hundred years ago to the Greeks.

What we needed was the Messiah to come.

To come and lead us into battle.

If I ever prayed, it was for the Messiah to come.

I didn't talk to God much, except for that.

I was a Jew, but I wasn't very religious.

When the word came that there might be one who was he, I went to find him.

He was in Galilee, at the Sea. So I left Cana, my home and went searching. The day I caught up to him, he was in Capernaum.

I followed behind in the crowd for awhile.

But nothing was either what I expected or wanted.

Yet he was fascinating!

I couldn't turn loose!

I just followed around behind him like a little puppy dog.

He did things that could only be done through the power of God.

He talked about God's kingdom, but it didn't exactly sound like what I dreamed about.

Oh there was plenty about justice and freedom.

But there was this peace, joy and love that were more important than anything else.

I just couldn't figure how you could have it all.

His teaching had a way of worming itself into your heart and then informing your mind. The longer I was around the more certain I was that he was the one.

His winsome strength dominated each of us who followed him from place to place, watching the miracles and absorbing the wisdom.

My fellow Zealots began to question me about him.

Would he?

Would he lead the army against Rome?

Would he free us from oppression?

I didn't know what to tell them.

Ernie Bein

Was he the one?

Well, yes.

I was becoming more sure of it every day.

Would he lead us into battle?

I wasn't sure.

I really doubted it.

Did he hate the Romans as did we?

Definitely not!

He didn't hate anyone!

I was confused, and so my words didn't help my friends much.

They wanted clear answers!

They had to be the right answers.

This man didn't seem to have the kind of answers my friends and I wanted.

It seemed as though everything he taught was aimed right at me.

He seemed to watch me more carefully than some of the others.

He had begun to pick a few to be a part of his closest group. One day I felt a touch on my shoulder. It was him.

"I want you to be one of my apostles."

"M - Me Lord?"

"Yes, Simon. I want you to be with me."

Of course I agreed!

Can you imagine.

No one had ever treated me as though I was worth anything.

Important people didn't even talk to me.

I was powerless.

I had no money.

I owned nothing.

There was nothing important about me. But suddenly I felt like I was worth something.

You see, the most important man I had ever met, or even knew about, wanted me to be one of his close friends.

Me!

He thought I was important.

No one else had ever thought so.

But he did.

The others with him - they were mostly important people. They treated me just like I was equal to them. They even treated me as though they had known me all my life.

I had never been treated with such respect before.

It made me think about myself differently.

I began to measure what I said!

I began to think about what I did!

Even what I thought about!

Was it worthy of an important person.

Was it something that someone who was worth something would do?

Would say?

Would think about?

I began to see the world differently.

Life wasn't so bad anymore.

As a matter of fact.

Life was good.

The crowds kept growing.

Most of the crowds were Zealots.

They were gathering, waiting for marching orders. Waiting for him to give the word to begin the war.

I became less and less convinced that anything they expected would happen with him.

That day on the mountainside he set things straight.

You could not plan to kill your enemies and follow him at the same time.

Armed violence was in complete opposition to his teaching, example and commandments.

"Love your enemies."

"Do good to those who despitefully use you."

"Retribution cannot happen if you are mine!"

Love, not hate, is the standard when dealing with enemies.

Well, a lot of folks didn't want to hear that. They wanted to keep safe their hate and anger against their enemies.

What he was teaching us was a new way to deal with life.

A different way from the way the world taught.

Even different from the way our Jewish tradition had taught.

He was teaching a new level of righteousness. A level beyond keeping a set of rules to a new kind of lifestyle of love.

As I think back, it was a great moment in my life when I met Jesus face to face. When he tapped me on the shoulder and the long distance admiration became a personal friendship.

I had known of him and about him.

When I knew him, not about him, it was a wonderful thing.

My worthless life was turned into something new and beautiful.

But the best part was still to come.

Ernie Bein

Growing in my relationship to him, growing in knowledge of him, growing with him as my companion and mentor, that was the very best.

Life was better than I ever thought it could be.

I remember the grand entrance into Jerusalem.

That was a day.

He took it right out of scripture.

Everyone knew what he was declaring when he rode into town on that colt.

We were enjoying the attention too.

I was enjoying the attention.

I could see a lot of my friends along the road and right through the East Gate. I could see it on their faces! Daggers and swords would have materialized out of the walls of Jerusalem if he had lifted a hand or said a word to call the men to arms.

But that wasn't what this was all about.

That wasn't what this revolution was all about.

This revolution was a revolution of the heart.

It was about a freedom of the soul - a freedom that chains and jails cannot touch.

It was about justice that was beyond judgment and retribution.

It had a better way than war and fighting to change things.

This was about changing the passion of men - from themselves to others.

This revolution was about changing lives.

It works!

He sure changed mine!

Ernie Bein

Chapter Nine

Zacchaeaus - the Chief Tax Collector

THE WITNESS:

Zaccheaus was a gentile, born in Galilee and serving the Roman government as a Chief Tax Collector. His religious background was pagan, but he had become significantly dissatisfied with his spiritual condition. He was a seeker. He was a very short man. Romans were short of stature, but they were generally taller than Zaccheaus. He bore all the "little man" stereotyped personality traits; struggling to be dominant and succeed, to be recognized and gain approval. He had the need to prove he was as good or better than any man taller than he. It was not good enough to be just a Tax Collector, he had to become the Chief Tax Collector. All of his successful struggle to dominate, achieve, acquire wealth, prove he could better bigger men, and of course, have women want to be in his company, did not fill the emptiness in his soul. When he sought what Jesus had to offer everything began to change for him.

THE TESTIMONY:

I had always been driven to succeed.

To excel.

And I have.

I most certainly have!

I had, by my own power and cunning, done better than men twice my size.

I had done everything I had ever wanted to do.

I was, by all reasonable standards, a success.

A very big success.

I had a beautiful home, a great deal of wealth and respect from everyone, except those radicals who try to ignore the realities of life.

When you are in a conquered land, it is only prudent to be the friend of the conqueror.

As I was saying, I had respect from everyone who counted.

I could not do anything about people tilting their heads down to look at me. But I could and did create the circumstance that caused those heads to nod in deference.

They may not have liked me. But they did show respect.

Jericho had always been my home. I was one of the majority population - that is, I was Gentile. Only about one in every five or six of the population was Jewish.

You see, when a conqueror took over a nation there were people moved out and others moved in.

By force.

"Redistribution of the population" it was called!

It was a military tactic.

"Redistribution of the population" helped control large numbers of people with small numbers of soldiers. The trick was to put strangers in with other strangers and take the home folks off to be strangers somewhere else.

It worked most of the time. Always for a little while. People were so busy fighting each other, or at least distrusting each other, that the conqueror was safe.

Jericho was a busy place.

A cosmopolitan community.

Much commerce.

Differing groups and attitudes.

The Roman Road, that crossed the Jordan River near Jericho at the Ford of Bethbara, ran right through town.

A thick jungle grew from our city toward the Jordan.

We were at the edge of the fertile, moist earth of the Jordan valley that supported lush vegetation.

There was barren wilderness between Jericho and Jerusalem.

The passage between Jericho and Jerusalem was perilous.

Robbers waited. Hiding in the rocks, ready to attack any prosperous looking, lonely person.

It was best to travel in groups large enough to ward off any attackers.

The Road to the Jordan was less dangerous, mainly because it was so heavily traveled.

There were jungle animals, lions and such, that might attack a lone traveler there also.

It was clear that there was safety in numbers traveling to and from our city.

There were no Roman soldiers stationed in Jericho, but they were moving through regularly.

We were an important place.

That is why, even though Jericho had been destroyed many times through history, it always got rebuilt.

We had deep wells which makes us an oasis on the edge of the desert wilderness. We are on the travel route to the most important places in the world.

So we always got rebuilt.

With such a busy and important city, there was a lot of money and my business was good.

I had ten other Tax Collectors working the area.

I, of course, got a part of what they collected.

Then I had my own accounts.

I did very well.

It was a good living.

A very good living.

A very good living, indeed!

When you have an army to lean on anyone who does not pay up, you never have too much trouble collecting. I didn't have to worry about an inventory as did the merchants. I just had to keep track of theirs.

Ernie Bein

I had been doing this for years. I was considered a prominent citizen of Jericho. I was very well known. I was also very rich.

Some criticized the collection of taxes as immoral.

But that was just business.

You got whatever you could get. What was fair, was what I said was fair. If it was more than what the Romans want by ten times - so what?

I'm the Tax Collector.

The **Chief** Tax Collector.

I was in charge of all of that.

They all did what I said.

I got as much as I could get. Any way I could. It was all perfectly legal. I was the law, you see. What was fair, was what I said was fair.

I really didn't care about the attitudes of the people about me and what I did. If I heard someone complain about me or the taxes, I would just raise their taxes even more.

Sometimes, I would raise the tax just because I wanted to raise the tax.

I enjoyed those tall men begging me to lower the amount.

I had power.

It felt good.

I had everything I wanted. I had done everything I had wanted to do.

Others may have felt I wasn't moral, but I didn't care.

I was very religious, you see, so I didn't care what they said. I had my own code of morality. I just keep my business and religion separated. Each in it's own place.

I had been in nearly every temple in the whole of Judea, the Decopolis, Caesarea Philipi, Samaria, and Gallilee. I had burnt incense and offered sacrifice to every god I knew about.

Every one, of course, except the Jewish Yahweh. Those narrow minded Jews wouldn't let me in their Synagogues or Temple.

Arrogant fools!

Those Jews were arrogant fools!

Narrow minded beyond imagination!

They were self important Jewish jackasses!

But I didn't care.

I had other places to go.

I was a very religious man.

I had many gods.

I had celebrated one festival after another in every religion I could find.

All of that is supposed to give a man peace of mind and a sense of well being.

It never worked for me.

There was always something missing.

I kept on pushing when I didn't know what I was pushing to get or be.

I was too religious to limit myself to one god, like the Jews did. I was more religious than they.

At least that was my first thought.

But later, out of desperation, I would have tried that Jewish thing too, if they would have let me.

I was not a Son of Abraham, that is, of Jewish lineage.

So I would have had to go through a lot of preparation before I was allowed to worship Yahweh.

I was told their god, Yahweh, lived in the Temple in Jerusalem. Of course the Samaritans said the same god lived on Jacob's Mountain in Samaria.

Either way I wasn't worthy to worship him, they both said.

I would have to begin by giving up all my wealth, stop being a Tax Collector, mourn for my sins by wrapping myself in burlap and rubbing ashes all over my body to make my skin sore and then take training on how to be a Jew.

Finally I would have to be circumcised.

That has got to hurt.

The ashes were nasty and disgusting - but THAT - has got to be painful.

I didn't want to do that.

I absolutely did not want to do all that.

They made it clear that they really didn't want me to become a Jew anyway.

Arrogant and self important were they!

It wasn't worth all that to be a Jew.

They were a conquered people, for goodness sake!

How did I know that my life would have the peace and joy I sought, if I did all those things?

So I didn't do anything about becoming a Jew.

But I was very religious.

I did all the right religious things for every other god or religion. I kept all the rituals and did all the rites.

But I didn't feel the peace.

I didn't have the sense of well being that I was supposed to have.

Until I met this Pharisee from Galilee.

From Capernaum to be exact.

He was causing quite a stir.

Everyone was talking about him and great crowds were following him everywhere he went.

He was more than an ordinary Pharisee.

He was special.

Ernie Bein

Now don't misunderstand, he had all the Pharisee's beliefs: same scripture, same sense of eternal life, same sense that what we do every day is more important in our relationship to God than what we do in Synagogue or Temple, or in any religious ceremony.

To the Pharisee, religion was on the streets and in the fields.

It was in daily lives and with each other.

Where this Pharisee and the other Pharisees differed was about the rules.

Pharisees had rules for everything.

They really loved the people, but were willing to require rules of behavior that were too complicated and too hard for ordinary people to do.

Everyone messes up on something, so no one had a sense of well being, because they were afraid to do or say anything for fear they would make a mistake.

Then there were the clever ones who knew how to use the rules to their selfish advantage.

They would use what they wanted to use to avoid doing the right thing.

Sometimes the Pharisees seemed not to care as much about the right thing as they did about the rules.

This Pharisee, his name was Jesus, had a different approach than that.

He didn't care what mistakes you had made, he offered hope anyway.

He talked about mercy and forgiveness.

THE SHADOW DANCERS

He said it didn't matter what you did, God was bigger than your mistakes if you let God be your God.

A Tax Collector at Capernaum had just walked away from the Tax Desk and just left money laying around!

He left people who were in line and not taxed just go on through without paying.

He did it in order to follow this man.

Sirus, the Chief Tax Collector of Galilee, was so angry he made himself sick. He laid in bed, his mouth all twisted up to one side, arm just dangling there. He still doesn't walk so good.

Sirus just didn't understand this "fogiveness" thing Jesus talked about.

Someone told him he should go see this Jesus, who had the power to heal. Sirus' crutch was broken over the poor fellow's head for suggesting it.

Jesus certainly created a lot of stir among the Tax Collectors, to whom he seemed to be very kind.

So I was really interested in seeing and hearing this Pharisaee.

I heard about his coming through Jericho, and, like everyone else in town, I wanted to see him.

Just to see, with my own eyes, who everyone was talking about.

The streets were very crowded.

I kept trying to get a place to look through and see, but I had a hard time.

Ernie Bein

You see I'm short.

Very short.

I couldn't look over anyone's shoulder, so I had to find a place between people.

Folks weren't helpful.

You see, when people don't like taxes, they don't like the Tax Collector.

When they hate taxes, they hate the Tax Collector.

I made them show respect, but I never captured their hearts.

Didn't want!

Didn't try to!

So I didn't get help or sympathy from the crowd.

I was determined they were not going to keep me from seeing this man.

I ran ahead to a tree that had limbs that hung over the street. I climbed up and scooted out on the limb.

It must of been a humorous sight; me dangling with my arms and legs wrapped around the thick branch hanging down and gawking over my shoulder at the parade.

He stopped right underneath me and laughed out loud. I was prepared for him to make a joke of me, looking as foolish as I must have looked. Short and getting old and fat and hanging out of a tree.

But he didn't.

THE SHADOW DANCERS

He called me by name.

He had this strange little smile on his face and he called me by name.

His lips just sort of curled up at the corners.

And he called me by name!

At first he just stopped and looked, in a very amused sort of way, and laughed.

Then he called me by name.

We had never met, **but he called me by name.**

Well, I guess I was kind of famous around here.

Or maybe **infamous** is a better way to put it.

But all the same, I was surprised he knew my name. This man everyone has been talking about knew me by name.

But that wasn't the biggest surprise.

"Come on down, I must stay at your house today."

At my house?

It would have been more appropriate for him to stay with another Pharisee.

That was the usual.

That was how things were done!

A traveling Pharisee would be housed in a town by the Pharisee who taught at the local synagogue.

Ernie Bein

But with me?

A Tax Collector?

This was quite a surprise - for everyone!

It was a great honor for me.

To be chosen by him in such a public and specific way.

He didn't seem to see me as a Tax Collector.

Or an old man hanging out of a tree.

He seemed to see me as a man of worth and significance.

I wasn't even a Jew, a Son of Abraham.

Yet, he clearly accepted me where I was.

He accepted who I was and what I was.

There were no terms and conditions about what I had to do to be worthy of his company, or his theology, or his friendship.

He stripped away all the stuff that was so important to everyone else and looked right into my heart.

I found the peace I had been searching for as I looked down into his warm, smiling eyes.

I had a sense that I would be all right, no matter what happened.

I swung down from the tree and happily led him to my home.

I was painfully aware of what they were saying about him because he was going to my home.

They were right!

I wasn't worthy of his presence.

I began to take stock of myself.

I had to admit, to myself, things I had pretended were not true.

If I was going to have him as a friend, things had to be different.

I was going to have to be different.

Not because he told me I had to be different.

Because I wanted to be different, so I could show him how much I wanted to be his friend.

So I wouldn't bring shame to him by his being my friend.

Truthfully, I knew I had cheated some people and taken advantage of others because of my power.

I knew that I had been dishonest, no matter how I had denied it in the past.

I could fool others, but I could not fool myself,

or Yahweh,

or Jesus.

I knew what I had done and what I had to do to make amends.

So after I saw to all the necessary matters a good host sees to, like having a servant set about washing the feet of Jesus and his people, I got busy.

I excused myself, saying I had to see to dinner.

That was a lie.

My servants were preparing the meal, while my stewards and I sought out persons I knew I had cheated. He knew I didn't have to see to dinner, but he just smiled at my lie and rested until I returned.

There were a lot of surprised expressions around Jericho that afternoon. We didn't get to all of them, but we did get a start. A very good start.

When we were at table, with Jesus at the place of honor, I turned to him and told him what I was doing to live a life more appropriate for a friend of Jesus. Half of all I had was going to go to the poor. I was returning four fold anything I had received by cheating.

He smiled and said in a loud voice so all could hear "Today salvation has come to this house," then he pointed to me and said "since he also is a Son of Abraham."

There was shock on the faces of all the guests.

There was a noticeable draft as all the Pharisees sucked in wind.

You could hear the buzz of those standing at the windows watching us.

He didn't talk about rules.

He didn't talk about all my mistakes.

He didn't talk about who my father was.

None of that was important.

What was important was that he and I were friends and that I returned the love and true respect he gave to me.

So he used that old cliché - "Son of Abraham" - used only to describe Jews and Jews alone - to describe me.

"He TOO is a son of Abraham."

Then he said something that made everyone think.

"For the Son of Man came to seek and to save the lost."

That surely wasn't very religious.

I guess I wasted a lot of time trying all that religion stuff.

Religion attempts to become worthy in order to get the love that he gave me freely.

That he gave everyone freely.

Religion is a weak attempt to achieve through rules and requirements what Jesus gave me as a free gift.

Jesus freed me to do what is good and right because I want to do it in order to show everyone I am his friend.

I want to live the way he teaches we should live, because I will not betray my friend.

He did it by loving and accepting me, just the way I was.

Because he did, I am not the same!

I will never be the same!

Ernie Bein

Chapter Ten

Mary - A Samaritan Woman

THE WITNESS:

A sad and defeated woman, she has had to be an opportunist to survive. She knew the things necessary for a strong spiritual life. She had long ago lost the energy to achieve it. Neither she nor others felt she was acceptable to the Lord. Like most Samaritans, she didn't have a lot going for her. Her self esteem was very low. She was more amoral than immoral, doing what she had to do to survive. She was amazed by one who knew all about her, but did not condemn her. Instead he gave her hope. Hope that she could receive the living water he had to offer. Even she.

THE TESTIMONY:

It was easy for people who had never been hungry or scared, to decide what was right and what was wrong.

I was taught the Law in my father's house.

When I was a child in my father's house I knew we were poor. But I was loved and felt safe.

I knew that my father would take care of me.

Life didn't turn out the way I thought it would.

As a child, I had looked to the Mountain of Jacob every day with a hopeful and joyful heart.

I have prayed to the Lord God of Jacob every day.

I dreamed of walking upon God's mountain as did Jacob.

I had dreamed of seeing the ladder with angels climbing up and down.

I dreamed of angels around and over me. Bright, happy and friendly spirits, that knew and loved me the way my daddy did.

I was taught right from wrong.

I was taught the difference in beliefs between Jews and Samaritans.

We were right!

At least I was convinced we were.

I was born a Samaritan.

That is who I am.

I know what the Judeans and Galileans say about the Samaritans.

"How does a Samaritan drive a nail? - With his head, of course."

"How does a Samaritan know which way is home? - He asks his donkey."

"How does a Samaritan count? - He doesn't because he doesn't know his fingers from his toes"

Despite the jokes **WE WERE STILL CHILDREN OF ABRAHAM!**

We started off as the nation of Israel when Solomon's Kingdom was split by his sons.

We were conquered by the Babylonians and the Assyrians.

Ernie Bein

Then by the Egyptians.

We did not have a walled city to stand within from enemies.

Megiddo is a military fortress.

There is not enough room for all the people there.

So every country that has a large army has conquered us.

All of our very best people -

our smartest,

our strongest,

our most skilled,

our most talented-

were carried off to Babylon, Assyrian, Egypt and other places to use their minds, strength, skills and talents to build those nations.

We are descended from the least smart, least skilled, least strong, least talented that were left.

So our neighbors make fun of and even despised us.

We live with that.

But we had as much right to be God's people as anyone else.

I was poor, but there was one thing I had - that I owned - that belonged to me and me alone.

The one thing I had, that was my own, was my tear jars.

THE SHADOW DANCERS

Tear jars were made with a little lip that was curved to fit under your eye. When you cried, you could catch your tears and save them.

Tears are precious.

They are the product of the best and worst times of a person's life.

I cried when I fell and cut my knee and saved my tears.

I cried when I felt lonely and afraid and saved my tears.

I cried when I curled up with my brothers and sisters at night and felt warm and safe. I saved my tears then, too.

I cried when I left my father's house and saved the tears.

I cried on my wedding night and saved the tears. I cried when my husband died and saved the tears.

The older I got, I had more tears of sadness than tears of joy, but I saved them all.

Those tear jars were the essence of my life. I carried them with me from place to place in a bag of goat skin thrown over my shoulder.

I grew up pretty.

I grew up fast.

I would have been glad not to have, but I did.

So I got married very young.

The wife of an older man in our town died. He came looking for a new wife. I was young but very pretty so he took me.

He gave my father a big dowry.

Ernie Bein

A very big dowry.

I was proud that our family could do well from my marriage.

I looked forward to being the wife of a man who would take care of me as my father had.

So I was married.

You see, in our way of life a woman must belong to some man or she is without a living. So I was pleased when I married a man of some worth.

My husband gave me a flask of nard, a fragrant ointment, the perfume of the wedding bed. He gave me a generous quantity of it and liked me to use it when I came to him on our bed.

My joy was short-lived. My husband died two years after we were married.

As is right, all that belonged to my husband became his eldest son's. Since I was not his mother, he had no responsibility or obligation for me.

He did not choose to allow me to stay.

His wife felt I was too young and pretty to live in the house that was now theirs.

All I had left was my flask of nard and my tear jars in my little goat skin sack.

I decided to seal the flask and save the nard for a man who I would love as much as I loved my first husband.

I never found one.

In the usual sense, at least, I never found one.

I was turned out.

I found myself with no place to go and no one to care for me.

I was ashamed to go back to my father's house.

He did not need another mouth to feed. I could not become a burden on him.

Most of the dowry was gone, so he had a struggle to live and keep those still in the house.

So I did what I needed to do to live.

Another man wanted me for wife. I was still very pretty. I became the man's second wife.

Of course SHE was always first.

She never let me forget that. She made life miserable for him and me for about ten years.

Finally, he gave me a letter of divorce.

It was a blessing I was barren.

Life was hard enough taking care of myself.

I could never have cared for children.

I guess the rest of my life has been just more of the same.

I was always able to find a man to take me in, to take care of me.

What else was there for a woman like me?

Ernie Bein

I am not proud of it all.

Neither do I apologize for it.

I was not sure of what was moral or immoral anymore.

One way or another, I have always been able to find a man to take care of me.

I have not felt loved for many years.

If I have survived, the price has been high.

Very high.

I wonder if it is not too high.

There had been an emptiness in me besides the emptiness in my belly for a long while.

More than hunger.

I felt dry and barren inside.

I felt as though my very soul was a wilderness.

I was a lifeless desert.

I hungered for a different life.

A life where I could respect myself again.

I wanted to go home to my father's house, but I never could do that.

I could never go home to my loving father.

I never dreamed of climbing Jacob's Mountain anymore.

THE SHADOW DANCERS

I imagined that if I tried to go up that sacred mountain God would send a lightning bolt to burn me to a black cinder.

I was frightened to ever see, let alone meet, an angel!

When I did think about angels, I didn't imagine them with smiling faces or hovering around me in joy.

Then one day everything changed for me.

It started like all the other days, stale and left over from the night before.

I went to the well late as was my custom. It was easier for me if the other women were not there. They all went to the village well in early or mid morning. Most of them sort of met and talked together. Much of the talk was about me. It was better if I wasn't there. It was more comfortable for them and especially for me. I got there about noon.

He was there resting by the well. He looked right at me. That usually didn't happen in public. Men didn't stare at women. Especially if they were alone in a public place. He did. But not the way men look at women like me.

It wasn't **THAT** look.

It was a "kind" stare.

I didn't like for men to stare at me any more.

I did when I was young and liked being pretty.

But I didn't like it any more. It made me feel unclean.

I didn't mind the way he stared at me.

Then he talked to me.

He actually talked to ME - a Samaritan woman.

Most Jews would choke before they would pass a respectable word to a Samaritan.

Never would they speak to a Samaritan woman!

Never!

It just wouldn't happen.

It started by his asking me for a drink of water, and I wasn't very polite.

It did not take him long to let me know he knew all about me.

At first I wondered if this might not be a cruel joke some of the town folk had planned.

I was soon convinced that this was no joke.

It didn't matter to him. He knew it all and it didn't matter.

He still looked at me kindly.

He still treated me with respect.

He still acted as though I was a human being.

No one had been this nice to me in years.

Not in many, many years, had anyone been that kind to me.

He cared.

He really cared about me.

I feel loved again.

No, he didn't touch or fondle me.

Or even hug me.

There was always a lot of space between us.

But I felt loved again by one who seemed to live love.

I feel love again!

Every minute of every day of my life!

Despite my mistakes.

I feel as though I am loved again.

I feel as though I have come home to my father's house.

He talked about happy things.

He talked about a fresh clean water that would fill my soul and refresh it's lifeless desert.

He talked about eternal life living in the loving house of the loving Father.

About a loving Father God, who was wherever his children were and loved them no matter what.

The God of Abraham, Isaac and Jacob was his Father God.

I believed him.

No.

Ernie Bein

I believe him.

I ran back to the town and told everyone.

They were amazed.

They went to see for themselves.

Not all of them really understood.

But then not all of them had known loneliness and despair the way I had.

But no matter what I told them about Jesus, I made sure they found out for themselves.

You can debate theology, and I did.

You can argue about who has the right belief system, and I did.

You can convince yourself you can do anything and it is all right if it helps you survive, and I did.

You can sit and think about living a better life that you won't be ashamed of living, but never change, and I did that too.

What you cannot debate, argue with, make excuses for or ignore is the life experience of meeting one who is the Son of God.

I did that.

Oh, I really did that!

Praise God, I did that!

I pushed them all to get out to the well and meet him.

THE SHADOW DANCERS

By the time everyone got back out to the well all of his friends were back there too.

He came back to town and stayed with us awhile.

They all came with him.

We were changed by that.

Our little village was never the same.

I was never the same.

Somehow, I managed to get along without doing all the things I thought I had to do to survive.

I followed Jesus around to places where he was going or was staying.

I begged for food and occasionally got a few coins.

My reputation as a fallen woman preceded me everywhere.

I wasn't treated with respect by most people.

I didn't care, as long I could see or hear him.

I just kept trudging around the countryside after him toting my little goat skin sack of personal belongings.

At one place the arrogance of and intended insult by the Pharisee who was Jesus' host that evening was the talk of the crowd gathered outside the house.

Jesus had not been given the most merger of the amenities due a guest in someone's house.

He didn't even get his feet washed by the servants.

Ernie Bein

The Pharisee had invited Jesus only because he had to do so.

Jesus was a Pharisee and it was up to the resident Pharisee to give him food and lodging.

I was furious and pushed my way inside opening my sack at his feet.

I was weeping to see him.

I was weeping because he had forgiven me and set me free.

I was weeping because I loved him.

I was weeping because he was being treated shabbily by one who claimed to be righteous.

I began to break open my tear jars and to pour out my tears upon his feet.

I began to pour out the essence of my life upon his feet.

I began to pour out all that I was or ever had been upon his feet.

Not because my life was worthy, but because it was me and it was all I had.

I poured out all of me upon his feet and washed them.

I washed them with my tears, my life time of tears.

I dried them with my hair.

When they were clean and dry, I opened the flask of nard and smoothed it upon his cut and tired feet..

He had given me my life again.

THE SHADOW DANCERS

I had given back all that I was.

More than that.

I have found a man I loved more than my father,

or first husband

to whom I could give my perfume.

Ernie Bein

Chapter Eleven

Judas

THE WITNESS:

Judas was a wealthy citizen of Jerusalem, the second son of a socially prominent, aristocratic family. He received a limited financial dole from the family. As a very young man, he had been politically and spiritually aligned with the Sadducees. The murder of his father, a Priest, when Pontius Pilate came to Jerusalem, caused him to become a radical revolutionary. He immediately connected to the Zealot Party. A very new and very small splinter revolutionary group of urban guerrillas called the Sicarii also began to receive his loyalty. Their determination to overthrow Roman rule was what appealed to Judas. He was a courageous man, willing to participate in Sicarii murdering and sedition. He fed them money and information. He considered the Priests and Sanhedrin to be traitors who had capitulated with Rome. He had developed a passionate dislike of the Sadducees, who refused to stand against the Romans who had murdered Priests. A very bright, clever, but arrogant man, Judas was impatient. He wanted to control things so they would happen according to his plan because he thought he was smarter than everyone else. He was a manipulator. His relationship with Jesus was very solid except in the area of who was in control. Judas truly loved Jesus and tried hard to be subservient, but he hated it. He related well to the poor and defeated, which fitted his personality, since they were more easily controlled and manipulated. But also, he was a compassionate man. He was genuinely burdened by the poverty and desperation he saw around him. He genuinely longed for the kingdom to come, but on his (Judas') terms. He didn't completely trust Jesus to get the job done right without his (Judas') help. He was a very complex man. Completely the opposite of the simple and transparent Peter.

THE TESTIMONY:

One must always consider the contextual circumstances of a dilemma, before one makes a judgment regarding the appropriateness of any action to be taken.

The context of our circumstance was aberrant.

The numbers of beggars at the gates increased daily.

The poor grew in quantity and squalor.

Our nation was at a pitifully weak spiritual state.

We were being bled dry by Roman taxes.

Jews were betraying Jews to please the Romans.

Our circumstance was aberrant.

The Priests, Sadducees and Aristocracy would do anything to appease the invaders. Their ineptitude was obvious.

It was a theatrical panorama of wallowing, one lower than the next, to see which might be less of an obstacle to the Romans in their quest to strip us of all we were and had.

They had even changed our nation from our lunar calendar to the Roman solar one. We had two celebrations of every feast and festival of faith. The first (based upon the lunar calendar) preceded the other by as many as four days. It was especially confusing at Passover when those loyal to our tradition celebrated on the Roman Tuesday night, which was the Jewish Friday. Then, four days later the "official Passover occurred."

All that was wrong, *was* wrong, because of those despicable little foreigners who even stood on the roof of Solomon's Porch and watched us as we prayed.

Indeed, our circumstances were aberrant.

Something had to change. That is why I acted.

Not everyone had the courage to do something, instead of whining in the wind.

There were enough of us, however, to make life more difficult for our oppressors.

We were beginning to make some progress. The Zealots, though mostly inferior in mental ability, were on the right path and I was going that direction with them.

Then I had begun to relate to a new group, the Sicarii, that had been spawned off of the Zealots.

They had the most effective approach. Daggers in the backs of soldiers would bring things to a boil. We needed to start an all out war.

Dead soldiers tend to make generals nervous. Nervous generals tend to act impulsively. Impulsive military actions usually brought tragedy for those doing so.

I enjoyed it.

I liked sneaking up next to a soldier, sticking my sicarea in his back and then slipping into the crowd.

I enjoyed even more the little charade I would then play. I would point to the fallen soldier and cry out against violence and any who would do such a thing.

Once, at Ceasarea by the Sea, I did such a convincing job that the authorities enlisted me to help interview people to see what they might have seen.

I became so good at all of that I began to be known as Judas of the Sicarii. Judas Sicariot. Judas the dagger man. We changed it a little so the Romans would not understand what it was with which I was being identified. We made it Judas of the Iscarii. Judas Iscariot.

I was very good at this thing!

I was much smarter than most!

I was too clever to get caught.

I always had an ingenious way of conniving so things got done right.

Then I discovered him.

I had met some of my friends in Jericho after I had that particularly pleasant trip to Caesarea.

I had left my sicarea in between the third and fourth ribs of a young Roman soldier. I faded back into the crowd quickly. Then I pushed myself through the crowd and began to decry the murder of the Roman.

I even thought of a lot of emotional things to say about that "sweet faced young man."

"Some woman's son!" I cried. "Who would do such a thing!"

His comrades, who were but a short distance away when it all happened, began to pat my shoulder and share with me their grief and anger over his death.

They asked me to help interview the crowd to see if anyone saw what happened.

Ernie Bein

I was confident that with me helping the interviews no one would remember anything.

They took twenty men from the market place later to be crucified.

I laughed all the way to Jericho about the way I played those stupid soldiers for fools.

I was not only wise and smart, I was clever as well.

Well, I was sharing this with my friends and we were laughing louder than we should have been laughing. It was not wise for us to be seen or heard together. We were on the roof of Simeon's house, enjoying some fruit and wine as we talked.

Simeon quieted us and then we heard the crowd walking past the house toward the Jordan. We could look down on them from the roof without them seeing us.

Alexander explained these were people headed to the Ford of Bethbara to hear this Essene named John. He was, according to some, the one.

After some discussion among us, we decided to go also. We broke up into two's and three's, so the Romans wouldn't see us all together and headed through the jungle on the Roman Road to the Ford of Bethbara.

I was really surprised by the crowd that was there.

They were all there to hear this wild man "teacher" at the river.

They seemed excited about it.

But there was little congruence to that mob.

There were People of the Land and Aristocrats.

There were Sadducees and Essenes. That was a wondrous combination.

There were many Pharisees, both Scribes and Rabbis, in the crowd also, which I found curious.

Personally I would never have called that crude fellow a teacher. He was of a priestly family, but he lacked the training and cognitive power of the Pharisaic teachers. If ideas were a windstorm, John the Baptist couldn't have bent a reed.

His content was trite, but his delivery was loud.

His attitude was angry.

What he said was true, if simple.

Too simple.

Much too simple.

Ridiculously simple!

I detest simple answers to complex problems.

He wasn't the important one.

Among the crowd was this Pharisee who was the center of a group of Pharisees.

I couldn't take my eyes off of him.

It was a congenial group with much laughter and pleasant nods between men who are both friends and colleagues. They all seemed centered on this one man. He was a Rabbi from Capernaum and was held in high regard by his companions, if their actions were any sign.

Ernie Bein

When he stepped into the water to be baptized we were all amazed and some strange things happened.

His companions were obviously caught by surprise. They looked at each other with such wonderment, one might have imagined they believed he needed no repentance.

Was he that righteous and special among the most righteous of our people?

Strange things began to happen.

There was thunder and a dove came out of the sky and lit upon his shoulder. I was not sure of what really happened.

I did know that it was him I was interested in knowing more about, not that loathsome, dirty cave dweller.

Jesus had everyone's attention from the moment he started down the bank.

He had class.

Distinction.

I had to wonder why he was there with this "Wilderness Wildman".

Just to see the two together was enough to tell who was the better man.

My friends and I had a lot to talk about, when we got back to Jericho and lounged around Simeon's roof.

I didn't see him again until he was in Jerusalem for the Passover.

I overheard him teaching under the canopy of King Solomon's Porch at the Temple.

Rabbis would gather there to teach and some would come to learn. After I overheard only few words, he had my full attention. I listened to his wisdom, his perception and his grasp of the Life Righteous. I was impressed.

Listening to him convinced me.

I followed him back to Galilee.

I asked questions and was amazed at his answers.

He spoke with a certitude that lacked arrogance.

He just knew what he was saying was right.

I knew what he was saying right.

I had found the one.

I had become one of his closest followers. He picked me to be one of his special men.

I was smarter than all the rest. Somehow Jesus seemed to know my mind about everything.

I never lost contact with the Sicarrii.

I continued to help them in any way I might.

We needed them to be a little less aggressive at the time. I could control that since I still provided them with finances.

Especially after I had control of the treasury of Jesus followers.

I was trusted with the money box!

Ernie Bein

That gave me a chance to occasionally reroute some of the money to the Sicarii. They needed it more than we did.

Well, after all it was all for the same purpose.

Anyway!

I knew he had the answer.

I never felt he knew or understood how to apply himself to the political milieu. He seemed to completely ignore all of that sort of thing.

He didn't seem to grasp the importance of it all.

He never seemed to be looking for the right opportunity to use his power. He just kept on keeping on like he was following some plan.

I followed him for three years.

It wasn't easy.

It was good!

I was privileged to be among his closest friends.

We traveled together.

We ate and slept together.

We shared dreams and hopes and listened to his dreams and hopes.

We learned more being with him than we did listening to him.

He liked sleeping under the stars. Even when he was at Jerusalem, he never spent a night in the city. He always went out the East Gate and up the hill to a grove of olive trees. It was on the hillside above the tombs and overlooking the East Gate. It was at the top of the hill next to the road to Bethany.

What a sorry lot followed him.

The biggest crowds were of the People of the Land. They were spectacularly poor and ragged.

Then there were the others, about one hundred and ten of them.

They stayed with us after the crowds had left. Some were Pharisees and there was an Essene or two. Some were not even Jews. Some were rich. Many craftsmen. Some were young and some old.

There was a group of about twenty women with them.

Not whores.

They were respectable women.

Some with their husbands.

All with the permission of their husbands or fathers.

They were a blessing.

They took care of all the little details men aren't good about. They were strong financial supporters of our ministry with Jesus.

I was impressed with the way in which the right people and the right circumstance always seemed to be there for us.

It was like God was watching over us and sending what we needed.

Most of the people who were among the disciples were ordinary, but not common people.

Ernie Bein

Although they were better educated than the crowds, they were not the brightest and the best by any means. But they did things with and through Jesus that were notable, to say the very least.

When we were sent out, seventy of us, two by two, the most marvelous things happened in our hands. In the hands of all of us.

They were men like Mattias and Stephen and Justus and Joseph. Good men and true, who had decided to follow Jesus and do what he commanded.

I didn't think anything could get much better than all of that until the kingdom came.

Human lives were made better!

What a joy it was!.

The inner group, the Apostles, the group I was a part of, was a diverse and interesting group.

They too were good men and true - if a less than titillating company.

Poor Peter was such a bore.

John was a little fool; a spoiled teenager always wanting to know what he was going to get.

Thomas couldn't understand what he couldn't see.

Not a challenging conversation among them.

They were the quintessence of boring.

But it was an exciting time in spite of such boorish company.

What great crowds and wonders we beheld every day!

THE SHADOW DANCERS

The masses were moved beyond imagination by his words.

So if I had to tolerate people around me with whom I never would have been associated otherwise, it was worth it.

There were so many sick healed that I lost count. The sick and poor had someone to make their lives different at the snap of his fingers.

The spiritual life of the nation was being awakened.

He was the one.

THE ONE!

His connections went all the way to the top.

Time after time he had the crowds in the palm of his hand. All he had to do was close his fist and he could have taken it all.

But not him.

He was too slow to take advantage of the political situation.

He didn't seem to be bothered by the disappearing crowds.

I began to get concerned about the lack of the crowds at first, but then I remembered the teachings about the Messiah.

If anyone stood against the Christ, the Son of God, the Lord God Almighty would send an army of angels to destroy them.

We were going to be freed by spiritual avengers.

It had taken me a while, but I finally figured it all out.

My posturing with revolutionaries was a waste of time.

No need for Zealots or even Sicarii.

A spiritual army of angels would destroy the enemies of God's people.

Then we went to Jerusalem again.

The day we entered Jerusalem was awesome.

He had them all on his side.

The cheering still rings in my ears.

I remember it all.

They lined the road all the way down from Olivet through the East Gate.

Everyone knew what his being mounted upon the colt of an ass meant.

They had heard the stories from scripture.

He was declaring himself.

When people ran out of clothes to throw on the road (remember nakedness was a sin for us, so people could only go so far) they tore the branches off of trees and threw them on the road.

What a thrill!

I thought the kingdom was about to come!

Simon was nodding and grinning to his Zealot friends in the crowd.

I wanted to tell Simon that the Messiah had no need of human armies.

But then, I knew he knew that, even if his friends didn't.

I dreamed of the angelic hosts sweeping from heaven and destroying the enemies of Israel.

I was dreaming about that as we marched right up to the temple with him. He set the stage for a full scale revolution that day. It was an amazing sight!

Hypocrites and doves flying everywhere!

Tables toppled and pens opened!

It wasn't just those strong arms and that broad back of his that caused them to run.

No, no!

"My Father's house" he said. "**My** Father's house."

And they all believed it.

All believed it!

But after that, all he did was teach and heal, and the moment passed.

He could have marched right into Antonius and run off the Roman Army if he had wanted to do it.

Instead he went back to Olivet for the night and returned the next day to teach and heal.

I became very frustrated.

Ernie Bein

I understood that something had to be done.

My man Jesus needed some help.

He simply didn't understand what had to happen.

He shouldn't sit back and wait, something had to be done.

Jesus needed a facilitator!

He needed one bright enough to carry out a plan that would bring about the kingdom.

Jesus needed me.

So I decided to work it out.

It was a simple plan.

Everyone knew the teachings of our childhood.

God would send his Son.

Any who would resist the Son would have to answer to the angels God put in charge of him.

Any attempt at doing him harm would be met by an onslaught of vengeance from heaven above. An army of angels would descend upon and destroy any such perpetrators!

All we had to do was manipulate the Romans into a position where they would try to do him harm.

I had to guide those stupid Priests through it.

They were already afraid to take him out and stone him for blasphemy for fear he **was** the One and they would have to face the wrath of God.

I explained how they could trick the Romans without the Romans knowing they were being tricked. I explained that they couldn't lose.

I told them that if he wasn't the Messiah the Romans would succeed in killing him and it would be all over. But I never believed that would happen.

What I thought would happen was that as soon as they menaced him in any way God would send the Holy Army to destroy them and we would be rid of Rome.

Either way the Priests couldn't lose, I told them.

It wasn't as though I didn't have any concerns about this.

Some how I had this nagging worry that it might not go as I planned.

But when he gave me the seat of honor at the Passover, I gained courage. Then he said "What you must do, do quickly" and I knew that he knew.

I thought that he wanted me to do it.

I tried to make sure he understood that I loved him and was doing this to serve him. So I kissed him. A kiss could never be misunderstood, I thought.

That is what I thought.

But it didn't go right.

I just don't understand why God didn't act.

I had it all set up for him.

I planned it so well.

Ernie Bein

I knew what had to be done.

God messed it up!

Now Jesus is dead!

Jesus is dead and it is all over!

No one will ever believe a dead man was the Messiah. In a year or two no one will remember the name of Jesus.

Or mine.

He suffered so!

Oh, how he suffered so!

His poor shredded back!

I am so sorry he suffered so!

I loved him and I am the one that caused him to suffer so.

There is no longer any purpose to my life.

The only thing left for me to do is to join him.

Actually, it is God's fault!

God's inability to get the job done is the real culprit in all of this.

I just don't understand why God didn't do things the way I wanted.

Chapter Twelve

Caiaphas - the Chief High Priest

THE WITNESS:

Caiaphas carried the burden of the salvation of the nation on his shoulders - never thinking God could do it better. He was anchored in the tradition and was certain of his position. He did not have a very good sense of the spiritual as a personal experience. He dealt with all spiritual matters in terms of the community. The survival of the nation was the priority of his faith system. He resented any sense that Jesus might know or understand anything that he didn't. He saw all matters in terms of the political consequences.

THE TESTIMONY:

It is an awesome responsibility, being the Chief Priest!

That is my role in life!

It was my father's role in life before me.

And his father's before him.

I am the most powerful Jew alive today.

My family is the most powerful Jewish family in memory.

I make decisions that effect every person living in our nation, be they Jew or Gentile.

But with such power comes a terrible burden of responsibility.

Such authority requires impeccable judgment.

Ernie Bein

It requires crafty guile, if we are to accomplish all that is best for God's chosen people.

I have all the talents.

I perfected all of the skills necessary to do my job well!

I do do my job very well!

I must always be right in my decisions.

And I am!

My father, Annas, has been a great help to me.

God can rest secure in the knowledge that I run his nation well and care for his people wisely.

I have learned the art of capitulation well.

We have learned the art of capitulation very well.

As long as we are careful not to ask too much, the Romans have been willing to let us continue to do things as we have for generations.

Our traditions are important!

We tell people that we do things the way they were done from the time of Moses.

Actually we have been doing things this way for only about two hundred years.

Since the Maccabean revolt.

When we beat the Greeks and drove them from our land.

THE SHADOW DANCERS

We are descendants of the Maccabees.

We are the important aristocracy of our nation.

We do things the way our fathers have done them.

It is the way things were as we grew up.

We are comfortable with them this way.

We have everything we need in the Books of Moses, in our traditions and in our Temple Worship.

These things care for all the needs of the people of God.

Of course there are always some trouble makers who want to change things!

Those Pharisees, for instance.

They are a real pain!

They aren't satisfied with the Books of Moses!

Oh no!

They are intent upon including the Prophets and other wisdom scrolls as the basis of our faith.

They do not support Temple Worship with its sacrifices as the only appropriate form of worship for our people.

They have developed what is called "the Synagogue".

It has a worship centered upon prayer and teaching.

Ernie Bein

They are more interested in the lifestyles of the people, than they are in the careful attention to the religious rituals and feasts of our tradition.

The lifestyles of people are fickle!

You cannot depend upon people to do and be what God wants them to do and be!

All we have is our Temple rituals and feasts.

The Pharisees push for personal righteousness, when all that matters is the righteousness of the nation.

They have little or no understanding of what politics are about or the political pressures with which we must deal!

The Pharisees on the Sanhedrin are always a problem!

They just don't understand what has to be done to run things.

The political impact of masses of people coming to the Temple is important!

The Romans think twice before they attempt to do again what Pilate tried when he first came here.

High holy days make them nervous.

That is both an advantage and a threat to us.

As long as we keep doing what we are doing and there are no political threats, we will be fine.

Yet those Pharisees keep pressing us to change.

None was worse than this Jesus!

He would have had us pay more attention to how we treat one another than to our rituals!

Can you imagine!

Human beings are mean spirited creatures who are self centered and evil by nature! Why should those of us who have achieved righteousness in God's eyes worry about them? They will never appreciate any kindness we do for them!

All that matters is for us to fulfill the Law!

To make sure we do the sacrifices correctly!

To make sure the incense and offerings are burned correctly so that the sweet aroma of them reaches heaven and pleases the nostrils of God!

To make sure that the prayers and rites are performed correctly, with perfected dovening and solemn, pleading voices, so that they will be pleasing to the ears and eyes of God.

To make sure that the feasts are conducted correctly with the proper perspective and balance between food and the fear of God!

And of course that the people pay their tithes to the Temple as they should.

All this stuff about love and forgiveness was naive!

An eye for and eye is what the law says.

Only a fool would want to love his enemies!

He just didn't understand what life is about.

What difference does it make if people hate each other as long as they do the rituals right?

As long as they make the appropriate sacrifices?

As long as God gets the worship performance he has required, what difference can any of that make?

It really doesn't matter what a man is, it only matters what people think he is!

This Jesus should have talked to me before he started all of this stuff.

He could have learned a lot from me.

I could have helped him understand and conform to what we have been teaching for generations.

I could have saved his life.

Even the Pharisees could not agree with all he taught and did.

He wanted to change us, not to throw away the tradition, but to do more than it requires!

Can you imagine!

Few people can keep the law now, let alone go beyond it!

His teachings were too radical!

There was no reason for all of this!

No reason for change!

What used to be still should be!

What has worked for us for centuries will still work for us.

THE SHADOW DANCERS

What I teach, and my father before me, and his father before him, is all we need.

He stirred people up!

At times thousands of people had gathered to hear him.

He had no political understanding.

Such gatherings make Rome nervous.

The desire to change things makes Rome nervous.

When Rome gets nervous I have to find ways to calm them.

To assure them things are all right.

I don't like people making my job harder.

Making my life harder.

The truth is, he didn't really seem to care about or want to answer to any of us who are running things here!

He had just gone off here and there doing whatever he wanted as if he knew it all.

Like he had all the answers!

Like he had a straight line of communication with God or something!

He acted like he doesn't have to answer to anyone on earth!

He had made a lot of Romans nervous.

He had made a lot of Jews angry.

Ernie Bein

Very angry.

He should have been more careful over the years as he roamed around the countryside about who he made angry.

Folks tend to nurse their anger and wait to get even.

There was a lack of political awareness on his part.

He needed to learn to please everyone!

To make everyone happy.

Not to upset anyone!

You have to keep on smiling when you hate the person you are addressing.

You have to make people believe you are doing what they tell you to do, while you go about things your own way.

You have to deal around the corner to get things done that need to be done.

For instance, when he did what he did to the venders at the Temple, he made a lot of enemies.

He messed with people's business.

Their livelihood.

He wasn't very nice about it.

All the livestock got turned out.

The birds all flew off.

The coins were all over the outer court.

No one knew whose was whose.

Fights broke out between those trying to recover their money.

There were significant losses that day.

The venders and money changers lost a lot that day.

We lost a lot that day!

We've been working with those people for generations.

It has been very profitable for all of us.

The Temple made as much from those tables as did the venders.

They gave us a generous cut to do business here.

What they offered was an important service!

And the Temple profited.

God's house got a nice income!

We, of course, helped them out as well.

We hardly ever accepted the animals people brought with them on the busy seasons.

We would always try hard to find a blemish.

The people would have to buy an animal from the venders.

We always offered to dispose of the unworthy animal for the people.

Ernie Bein

If they allowed us to have it, we would run it into the venders pens.

All the venders animals were "preexamined and found worthy".

So a person could possible get back their own animal from a vender and it would be used to sacrifice.

Even when we didn't help them out, the venders were necessary and very profitable for us all.

Well, after all, the Temple is a business.

We made ends meet.

We had to make ends meet.

After all, can there really be anything wrong with something that brings money into the Temple?

The money changers were necessary and profitable too!

The Roman money had the image of Caesar upon it.

The Temple money had the image of the Temple upon it.

Roman money was used in the streets.

Temple money was used in the Temple.

The rate of exchange was arranged so the money changer, and the Temple, made a profit.

A nice profit.

As a matter of fact there was a very good profit in money changing.

We enjoyed a nice part of that profit.

All in all, the tables of venders and money changers in the outer court were very good thing for everyone.

This thing with Jesus wasn't practical!

The business in the court yard was.

It didn't interfere with anyone praying.

It helped people to sacrifice as they should.

The money made with all of this was more than worth the little twinges of conscience some prudish do-gooders felt.

He - that is Jesus - was just too idealistic - too radical, about this.

It made a lot of people angry.

It made a lot of people uneasy.

When it all started, the Romans poured out of Antonius onto the roof of Solomon's Perch and watched every detail.

They were on guard.

This whole thing made Jesus some enemies who would be waiting to get even.

The thing that he did to put us all on the spot was that entry into Jerusalem.

I mean, really!

How obvious can you get!

It was a clear declaration!

Even his close friends among the Pharisees couldn't handle that one.

He had every detail exactly the way the Prophet said it was to be.

He rode that colt.

His followers threw their clothes on the road so that the feet of the colt would not touch the ground while it carried him.

Then the palm branches were cut and torn from the trees and thrown on the road when the clothes ran out.

The parade with all of those "hosannas" through the East Gate told everyone that this man was laying claim to the Messiahship.

He was the Messiah come to claim his kingdom.

This wasn't exactly new.

That is what people have been saying about him for some time.

He had done nothing to discourage that talk.

He had asserted authority.

He had fueled the fire in the hearts of people who were claiming he was the one!

Now he out and out declared it!

I was not pleased.

We could have survived the Temple thing, but not on the heels of such a declaration.

I was not happy.

Rome was unhappily watching.

The events of the week just kept making things worse.

I had to do something.

I had to act decisively.

We could not let this thing go any further.

Yet we had to be safe in our action.

This Jesus was really a likable person.

But he presented a problem with which we had to deal!

We could have arrested him, take him outside the city wall and stone him for heresy.

What if it isn't heresy and he was the Messiah?

After all, he was either insane or he was what he says he was.

He surely had done things that no mere man could do.

We could not chance killing him ourselves!

Tradition says that anyone who tries to harm the Messiah will incur the wrath of God!

They will be destroyed.

An army of angels of death will swoop down and kill all who lift a hand against the Messiah.

So says tradition.

Ernie Bein

So if anyone was going to execute this Jesus it had to be the Romans.

Then if an army of death angels swooped down it would be all of Rome that was destroyed, not us.

You see, that is what is called smart politics!

It is a pragmatic solution to a difficult problem.

You set someone else up to do your dirty work.

Then you aren't in trouble.

They are!

It worked 250 years ago with the Teacher of Righteousness and the Greeks.

Those Essenes are still out there in the desert waiting for him to be resurrected.

It won't happen.

He wasn't the Messiah or they couldn't have crucified him.

God wouldn't have let them.

It has worked a number of times since and most of those who were called the Messiah are long dead and forgotten.

I am very wise.

If he was the Messiah, then he wouldn't die.

If he wasn't - well - it was better that one man die than a whole nation perish.

Then Judas came to us in his arrogance and self certitude and thought he was telling us what to do!

We didn't need his ideas! We already knew all of that. We had done so frequently over the past centuries. The bones of many would be Messiahs were bleached and dry along the roads of our nation. What we did need is his treachery to set up the situation for us.

Well, it didn't go as I thought it would.

Oh he died all right.

And that should have been the end of it all.

But it isn't.

All sorts of things have been happening that we cannot explain.

We don't understand what is going on.

And we have been blamed by Simon the fisherman for sinning against God.

That is preposterous!

We have done nothing wrong.

The Romans killed him.

Not us!

But all the same, Gamaliel gave us good counsel.

If this is of God, we best not fight it.

So far we are safe, so we best not fight it.

Ernie Bein

If it is not, it will pass.

I hope it passes.

I really hope it passes.

For the sake of us all, I hope it passes.

Soon.

About the Author

Ernie Bein is a retired United Methodist Pastor. He lives in Cincinnati, Ohio with his wife, Sharon. He continues to serve as Pastor of a small congregation, California-Columbia United Methodist Church. He served as an itinerant clergyman for 35 years, before retiring.

When he first read scripture seriously, he began to question the scriptural basis of some of our traditional Christian attitudes. The traditional description of Judas the traitor, of the Pharisees and of Jesus himself did not square with what scripture seemed to be saying. For nearly forty years he has studied, (his research bibliography includes over 100 titles) prayed and meditated with an attitude of discovery that has given him a different understanding of who Jesus and those around him were.

He was awaken to a possibility he did not want to accept when he heard Jim Flemming, Jerusalem Institute of Biblical Study, say that Jesus was a Pharisee. He studied everything he could find to disprove Flemming's assertion. He referenced scriptural data. He found that Flemming was correct and it changed the way he understood the stories of the New Testament.

He has become concerned about the reframing of scripture to suit theological postures. Therefore this book does not resonate with recent attempts to rewrite history and scripture in order to sanctify theological and sociological biases. Unlike what has come from radical liberal pens, this is not an attempt to throw out all that has been a part of the faith since the beginning. It is rather, an attempt to better understand it.

Printed in the United States
761600001B